# The Golden Web

## A New Partnership with Nature

# The Golden Web
## A New Partnership with Nature

*by*

Gwennie Armstrong Fraser

*Foreword by Dorothy Maclean*

FINDHORN
*Press*

ISBN 1 899171 25 8

British Library Cataloguing-in-Publication Data.
A catalogue record for this book is available
from the British Library.


Set in Garamond by Findhorn Press

Cover photographs by Simon Fraser
and Findhorn Foundation Visual Arts

Cover design by Posthouse Printing

Printed and bound by The Cromwell Press,
Broughton Gifford, Melksham, Wiltshire




Published by

# Findhorn Press

The Park, Findhorn,
Forres IV36 0TZ, Scotland.
01309-690582 / fax 690036
e-mail thierry@findhorn.org
http://www.mcn.org/findhorn/press/  *or*
http://www.gaia.org/gen/findhorn/press/

# Index

*For Simon, with my love*

*Acknowledgements*

*I am especially grateful to Thierry and Karin Bogliolo at Findhorn Press, and I thank them for all their help and support in bringing this book to publication.*

*I especially wish to thank my husband, Simon, to whom this book is dedicated, for our journey together, for our love of Nature and wild places out of which this book has arisen, and for sharing with me all the developments which led to the preparation of this book. I thank him for all his loving support, and for the thoughtful advice and encouragement he has given me through every stage of writing it.*

*I also particularly wish to thank my friends, Gill and John Guy Massereene-James, for our deep and enduring friendship. I am profoundly grateful to Gill for the picture work, which gathered the threads of my life together and led me to the heart of my journey. I thank her for her clear vision, her absolute commitment to the growth of consciousness and the development of all sensitivity, and for the encouragement they have both given me in following my own path.*

*I am also deeply grateful to Hope Tod, whose book* The Maze and the Arc of Light *I read at a turning point in my life and which stirred vital connections. I warmly thank her for the guidance she so kindly gave me which was greatly confirming. This book, too, has grown out of our contact and all that we have been able to share.*

*Finally, I wish to thank and acknowledge Mother Meera, for Her presence and Light in all things, Ashok, ROC and the Group for their wise counsel, inspiration and guidance throughout my journey, and the otters for leading the way in the first place.*

# Foreword

Most of us, when in an open mood, have taken a walk in the country and been awed by the intricate, minuscule beauty seen all around. Nature is amazing, and nature speaks to us when we listen. In this book we are taken on many such walks, and when the heart of nature, the devas, speak, we are told of the planet and of ourselves, of the wonderful qualities which they share with us and which resonate in us. We become more alive, consciousness speaks to consciousness, with worlds to share.

Gwennie puts into words what the core of nature is, and the messages awaken the angelic energies within us. When we live our lives in this awareness, we and nature support each other and delight together to enhance all life on the planet.

It is with joy that I encounter the viewpoint of the devas in The Golden Web, for always the essence, the devas, of nature communicate joy. Joy always rings forth through nature, and we can sense that joy in every minute detail of the natural world, resounding particularly colourfully in flowers. Nature openly displays the beauty and wonder of creation, but our modern eyes are so focussed on our problems, on our human relationships, on our past or future, that we are closed to nature's sights and insights.

When we look with sensitive minds at the infinite variety of nature, as primal people do and as Gwennie does, the inner core of nature can speak to us. When we love, our relationship with life opens us. This happens differently with each of us, for we are all unique beings. Within our uniqueness is our essence, and within each member of nature is essence, the same spirit, the same vital life force which supports us all. With love and appreciation essence communicates with essence.

I myself, after ten years of daily attunement to my inner reality, which I call God, was told by it that I had a job to communicate with the essence of nature. This first led me to the discovery of and attunement to the intelligence or devas of the vegetable world, and resulted in co-operating with them in the growth of a remarkable garden. The messages I received from the vast consciousness of the devas spoke of the oneness of all life, as do those in this book. They exude qualities which uplift and resonate with the deep qualities within each of us, expanding us to the vital forces innate in us all.

The perspective of life from the devic point of view is one of wholeness. Of course our human viewpoint of separateness and consequent mistreatment and domination of the natural world all over the planet, resulting in pollution of the air, the water and the earth, is obvious to them. They urge us to change. They give us a true vision of co-operation between the human aspect of nature and the unspoiled aspects of nature. Always they are positive, always they see solutions, always they see our potential for working with them. Imbued with their point of view, we cannot but change and together bring about more balanced planetary life.

It might seem that the devic point of view is too joyful and happy, and that humanity could not possibly live with the same attitude. They live in a realm close to God; like the elder brother in the story of the Prodigal Son, they have not left the Father/Mother's house. We humans have the choice to live likewise, and this book can help us to understand how we can do that. It can help us to become what we truly are, aspects of the divine expressing ourselves in the spiritual, mental, emotional and material worlds. Nature beckons to us, and with it we find wholeness.

Then we are inspired to work for the whole in ever more concrete ways, ways that flow through all dimensions, and we take our place as true stewards of our planet. This book points the way.

*Dorothy Maclean*
*June 1995*

# Introduction

This is a book about Nature, about the consciousness we share with Nature, and the importance of our relationship with Nature in the present ecological crisis. The book outlines a new partnership with Nature through messages I have received from the Devic level of consciousness within Nature. Devic consciousness is the vital force which gives life to all Nature's forms, creating the essential energies of the trees, the plants, the rocks and the elements which are woven together to produce life on earth. In their messages, the Devas describe the creative power of Nature, the energy and light with which they shape life, and the levels of consciousness we share with Nature in all places, at all times.

I have always felt Nature to be deeply alive. As a child, I knew instinctively that the trees, the rocks, the flowers and the streams were animated by the same spirit of life as human beings. Stepping into Nature I experienced this vital energy which filled the world with beauty and with countless shapes and forms. A love of Nature has accompanied me throughout my life, and it has always been in Nature and in wild places that I have most directly experienced the presence of the Divine.

One day, out of the blue, Nature communicated with me in a stream of consciousness different to anything I had ever experienced before. It came in the form of a crystal clear message. This experience was neither fantasised or imagined. It shattered my whole view of life, and led me to the realisation that Nature is truly alive, that it has its own levels of conscious life, and that through our own consciousness we are connected to all other life-forms. As a result, I was helped to see that human life is part of a unified whole, and that it is essential for us to develop ways of living sustainably and in greater harmony with Nature, in order to restore ecological balance.

A single transcendent spiritual experience can change one's entire view of life, and open the way to a new perception of reality. When these experiences began to reoccur, I started to record the Devas' communications in a note-book. It became clear to me that Nature had a wider message to communicate and that the messages were not for my own personal benefit. I eventually decided to publish these messages so that they could be read more widely, particularly in view of their significance to the environmental situation and the changes in consciousness that are taking place at this time.

There are many layers of understanding, and many layers of consciousness. The Devas' communications represent a distillation of the consciousness within Nature and of the patterns of life that shape physical matter and the world we inhabit. In their communications, the Devas call us to develop a much deeper awareness of Nature, of its profound beauty, intricacy and sensitivity, and to recognise and respect the life we share.

The spiritual connection which once linked humanity with Nature has been drastically eroded, and the consequences of this have already begun to threaten the balance of life on earth. Recent discoveries in physics, biology and mathematics point the way forward to a new understanding of the interdependence of all life. This book outlines the Devas' view of our relationship with Nature, and suggests how we may step forward together in a new and revitalised partnership, to begin the process of ecological restoration.

I believe that many people have a close relationship with Nature, and have had transcendent experiences in which they have felt closely connected to the rhythms and essential energies of the earth. I sincerely hope that the experiences I have described in this book will encourage others to experience Nature more deeply, and to acknowledge the great creative power and beauty which surrounds us everywhere. In their communications, the Devas encourage us to draw closer to Nature so that we realise its true value and experience it more powerfully in our lives.

I have always found Nature to be a source of fascination, wonder and inspiration. It has shown me that the essence of the Divine lies in all things: in the life of the greatest trees and the tiniest wildflowers; in the miracle of flow-ing water and constantly changing light. The energy of Nature is more detailed and all-embracing than I ever realised. The Devas have encouraged me to experience Nature as a flow of consciousness of which we are all a part. It is this flow of consciousness which binds all life together and infuses everything with the light of the Divine.

There will always be sceptics who say that there is no proof that we can communicate with plants, or that there is consciousness within Nature. This book does not claim to offer that proof, or set out to persuade anyone to change their viewpoint or belief. The events which I have recounted in this book could happen to anyone. I hope that sharing my experiences will help to nurture human sensitivity towards Nature, and that it will illuminate our true rela-tionship with Nature and the importance of protecting the divine web of life.

*Gwennie Armstrong Fraser*
*June 1995*

*chapter 1*

# The Light of Nature

I live at the edge of a wood, an old oak and beech wood tucked in a valley below heather moorland. The cottage lies in a hollow with the wood behind it and high ground rising steeply through meadows to the fells in front. In autumn the garden is full of wind-blown oak leaves, with silver droplets of rain caught on the uppermost ones, their round jigsaw shapes forming delicate layers where they gather against the stone walls. In fact, the cottage is set back into the wood and so it is part of it. The boughs of the beech trees spread behind the house like embracing arms and red squirrels use the climbing roses round the windows as ladders to reach the tree canopy behind. From the windows at the back of the house, I look deep into the wood to watch the whirling advance of autumn in showers of flurrying leaves, and snow-drops gently emerging from winter amidst quiet layers of the woodland floor.

Living by the wood is rather like living by the sea, for it is as vital, as changing and as wild as the sea, and it has its own life systems and intricacies. The power of the seasons evokes change in the wood in subtle ways, like new shoots which announce their presence early, so that one phase of life slips unobtrusively into the next, not abruptly, but woven together, a mounting rhythm like ripples gathering into persistent small waves, then reaching a great crescendo as the fullness of the season is revealed in all its glory, just as a wave merges and shatters, and ebbs into a new cycle. So the seasons come and go in perpetual motion, moulded by frost, sun, wind and rain, each season resonating with its own qualities and moods.

When a gale blows off the fells, the cottage is like a ship at sea, rocked by the swaying motion of tall trees. There is a sheltered, gentle stillness beneath the trees as the canopy absorbs roaring gusts high above, and thick trunks resist the storm. In winter, the frames of the trees stand quietly, and fragile details of the wood are silently revealed: the delicacy of purple, bare birch tips marbling the sky; the echo of running water; the movement of deer in sheltered pockets. Snow comes gracefully to the wood, painting angles of branches and stroking the trunks, while the fells spin in white squalls under leaden skies. The stirrings of spring are locked below ice, patiently waiting in inky darkness for wood anemones to open, like stars falling to earth, bringing the message of birth and renewal.

Living by the wood is like sinking invisibly into a pool of energy. I feel transparent and saturated in the details and intimacy of the wood. It is a sensation of losing physical density and walking lightly, unnoticed, alert only to scenes and details which grow in depth and texture, overlapping, familiar, and changing. Everything in the wood breathes the same air, and I breathe with it. The wood is full of presences, not just multiple names, but exquisite forms and colours, singular and startling in their individuality. My attention is seized by new developments. How could I not notice the new growth of a fern? When the ferns come, they begin life wrapped in the spiral of their fiddle heads, and the birch glade is full of them unfolding , striking up in shades of luminous green as sunlight filters through the trees. It is one display after another, miracles occupying minute spaces, the traces of lichen on the edge of a rock, wild garlic in shining pools of extravagant lace.

As spring passes into summer, the wood reverberates with bird song, and sweet, exuberant music is sent out from secret places shaded by green fans of rustling leaves. The sounds well up out of the wood in the early hours, for business begins at dawn as new sunlight warms and activates all corners of the wood. Energy is rising in the woodland floor as plants return: banks of dog's mercury and nettle, stitchwort and bluebell sweeping in brilliant pools of colour in dappled glades. And rising further still, bees form a throbbing halo about the trees, in loud swarms which gather in the lush expanse of new leaves.

At night, the garden fills with silver light and plants form strange blue shadows, caught still where night fell and left them standing. The sound of snipe drumming bubbles out from hidden reed beds, and the plaintive calls of curlews pierce the air as they glide over the heather moor to invisible nesting sites on the fell. All is gathered between these outbursts by the rushing of distant water, faint as the breeze snatches sound and returns it, louder and more acute; streams splashing on moss, the movement of river on shingle.

Summer warmth gathers in the meadow flowers and hangs in the night air. The meadow in front of the cottage becomes a moving sea of wildflowers, and buttercups rise to the surface like shoals of fish, turning in the breeze in shimmering, golden profusion. Everything is alive and present in these vibrant days, and secrets are concealed beneath abundant tangles. The fullness of summer gradually eases out into dreamy days. The moors are stained purple with heather and bilberry, alive with bees. Sheep call from patchwork fields across the valley, and high farms bathe in the glow of dusk. Summer lingers softly for a while, with long evenings slipping into stillness and cool as the sun edges itself below the horizon in a swollen, molten orb. And suddenly the air is chill, colours are distilled and quiet settles in the earth once again, as the curtain of approaching autumn drops in soft folds.

The beauty of Nature is encapsulated in the changing tapestries created by the passage of light and the movement of energy. Living at the edge of the wood gives a feeling of being part of the ceaseless ebb and flow of Nature, as it is endlessly shaped by the rhythm of the seasons. It is a feeling of being suspended somewhere in the midst of it, surrounded by fine strands weaving life together. The whole of Nature is ringing with life and consciousness, so full that my presence in the wood is one amongst millions. As I walk, I feel my sense of self melts, only witness to life in essential fragments: the chestnut glimpse of a wren; the clatter of a large raindrop through beech limbs after a shower; the mysterious, velvet lobes of a foxglove. It is a feeling of being joined to the wood, not remaining on the outside, but looking deeply into its multiple forms, allowing sensitive impressions to form, and exact details to imprint themselves on me.

I have always felt presences in Nature, and even as a child I sensed that Nature was charged with a mysterious energy which animated the earth with great power, giving character and life to its individual forms. I did not know quite what this animating spirit of life was, but I felt it tangibly in the things I loved to walk amongst and observe. It was always a strong feeling, tinged with awe, and rather magnetising. I sometimes felt as if Nature would burst in front of my eyes and then I would see this realm of energy, its unseen workings and presences. Instinctively, I understood that another realm lay within Nature. I respected Nature because of it and felt it was somehow sacred.

Because I had sensed these presences as a child, I assumed it must be possible to see them one day. Gradually as I grew up and came into contact with accounts of mystical and spiritual experiences, my interest was further awakened. These accounts confirmed that contact with other realms of consciousness is possible, and that in some traditions it is a normal part of human experience. I was quite content with what I had read and heard about the subject, for it confirmed what I intuitively understood. However, I wondered how these other realms fitted in with our physical, day to day reality. The fact that some people experienced them was one thing, but how and why did it happen? I felt there must be some establishing link, but that somehow these were experiences that only happened to other people, and I did not expect any such thing to happen amidst the normality of my own life.

The establishing link was the Devas. When I first heard Nature speaking to me through the Devas, the archetypal patterns and energies within the natural world, my love and experience of Nature since childhood came sharply into focus again with new meaning. I was not seeing the presences but hearing them. This brought the reality of other realms through into my own life with a single, profound realisation: that human life is part of a much greater field of consciousness, that Nature has its own levels of consciousness and intelligent forms, and that a flow of consciousness exists between humanity and Nature that allows mutual awareness and communication.

Consciousness is a force, a vital force which animates and links all levels of existence. It is active at many different levels and present in all spheres of life. The whole of life is a movement between changing levels of consciousness and awareness, embracing birth and death, our sleeping and our waking hours, and all aspects of our physical, mental, spiritual and psychic development. It is this central force which directs our evolutionary growth. Consciousness permeates life in varying degrees of light and intensity according to the level of its action, and as a single force it forms a continuum and a dynamic whole. The entire universe, including humanity and Nature, belongs to this central force and is in permanent relationship to it.

The Devic level of consciousness is a force of light and energy which exists throughout Nature. Devas belong to the plant, vegetable and mineral kingdoms and they exist in all places and in all things. They are essential energies composed of great light, and they are highly refined and pure in nature. Deva is a Sanskrit word meaning 'Shining One'. The Devas may be described as beings of light since they are the bodies of light and energy which encompass the growing formations of trees, plants, rocks, and also the elements. Devic consciousness thus embraces both organic and inorganic matter.

The Devas govern the formation, details and components of each individual species. They therefore represent the myriad forms of Nature and are beings which exist in light form to nurture the growth of all living systems. As such they are life-giving and they have their own consciousness. Since the Devas are involved in life formation, their nature is precise and exact. They bring together and focus the life energy of individual species, which is like a concentrated pattern and imprint. They are essential energy forms which contain the collective pattern of an entire species. These essential energies can be described as Devic essence, for they represent the total nature of a species and everything pertaining to a particular species is contained and gathered within the Devic energy and light body. Their consciousness is therefore highly evolved and represents the uniqueness of living forms.

The Devas always describe themselves in terms of light and they continually refer to the light of their realms. My contact with the Devas takes the form of messages transmitted in thought form from their level of consciousness to mine. One day I asked the Devas if they could describe the light of Nature to me. I was sitting on a favourite, large rock in the middle of a burn in the Scottish highlands. From this rock I could see downstream through waterfall pools and up the steep sides of a gully, to great walls of rock interspersed with trees and overhung with heather. If I reached out on either side, I could touch dense beds of moss and wildflowers at the sides of the pool. The Devas' reply was clear and detailed:

*All of Nature is an ocean of life-forming energy, and we are the tides and forces at work within the ocean, working to give it life, shape and form, and creating the seasonal and cyclical patterns. All life contains a basic energy or life-force. Each species, each individual plant, each detail of a stone, or a flower, or a grain of rock — the flow of water itself — is a moving interaction between these basic forces. We communicate to you a basic notion of energy. But it is important to understand that this energy is not a singular, independent entity — it is united and interwoven with ALL the energy at work in creation. Therefore we draw from the sea of light, the ocean of creation, to distil our imprinted patterns to an essence. This is the impulse of life which gives form to a particular plant or stone.*

*We are ceaselessly at work, shaping the flow of life. It builds. We are at work within an ancient matrix of energy which has already formed the landscape as you know it. We continue to build the detail, the cloth of the land which characterises the life of Nature which surrounds you. Everything is a manifestation of this force of life, an outward expression of essence, light and energy. We are the forces of subtle energy which govern the fabric and formation of life.*

*It is exquisite, intricate, detailed work. It is born of light, a light of distilled, pure energy. This is our source, to which we all belong. By the source we mean the greater essence from which we are derived and from which we receive our motivation and pattern to fulfil. The laws of Nature are complex, but we best describe it to you as a pattern of interwoven threads. Each strand is a strand of light and energy which weaves the cloth. It is so intricate, humankind has little conception of what lies beyond the outward form of Nature. But we are here, at work, ceaselessly creating life. We draw essence together — this is radiating energy which amasses and forms. Do you see? It is a shaping THROUGH energy. We draw together qualities.*

*And thus when you see us, if you do see us, you would see us as shimmering light, shimmering energy. You would be amazed by the beauty of our realms. You would know in an instant our luminosity, lightness and perfection. We reach forward to you in ways that you CAN perceive. Therefore perception of beauty, appreciation of form, quality, content — all these things bring you to an awareness of the fabric and substance of life, of which we are the central force. All of Nature is created by this central force, this central energy and light. It is the breath of life which sustains us all. Therefore we wish humankind to know us more*

*closely, to realise our interconnection, our inter-
dependence and our need to respect and mutually
benefit one another. In this, reality has to be recognised and understood for what it is, a much more
complex and detailed web of relationships than
has been understood.*

*We do not wish to give confusion or speak
in terms you do not understand. If you see beauty
in all Nature's forms, and know that beyond physical matter lie energy and patterns of light which
shape life, you have a basic understanding of what
our life-forms are. We have consciousness, different
to yours, but capable of transmission. Thus we
speak through to those who are receptive and can
receive the vibration of energy to which our
realms are aligned. We leave you with our light,
our joy, our blessings upon you.*

From the very beginning, the Devas taught me a new way
of looking at Nature and our relationship with it. I was told
that I was to begin to look at the connections between living things and the interrelatedness of energy in Nature. I
have always felt a sense of belonging whenever I step into
the purity of a wild place. I was now aware of the existence
of the Devas in all Nature's forms, but I was presented with
a further step. How could I as a human being perceive these
connections, and how was it all linked together? Asking these
questions inwardly, I began to explore the different levels
of consciousness which the Devas had opened to me.

When I first became aware of the Devas, it was like
seeing through a keyhole to a hidden garden in which everything was laid out in very beautiful, clear patterns. The Devas
referred to the 'inner forms' of Nature, and the messages I
received began to describe the nature of light and energy
with which they build life. Devic consciousness totally inter-
penetrates the physical, material world, and so the light of
Nature exists before our very eyes. It is a relatively small
change in our usual conscious state which allows us to
attune to this level of consciousness.

To begin with, I was shocked by how close this level of consciousness was. In an instant, Nature was infused with a new dimension of lightness, an all-embracing energy and unity, which was part of and in addition to everything with which I was physically familiar. Gradually I began to understand that the Devas do not belong to a secret garden which is only occasionally revealed to human beings, but that they lie within absolutely everything and are accessible at any moment in time. It was my own limited consciousness which had hitherto perceived them as belonging to a separate plane of existence. Contact with the Devas brought a new, expanded awareness of Nature which embraced more detail and greater appreciation of trees, plants and rocks as living forms with their own energies. This process did not replace my physical awareness of the natural world, for it was through daily contact with Nature in my immediate surroundings that I was able to communicate with the Devas in the first place.

In the early days of contact with the Devas, I certainly felt as if I were experiencing two different levels of reality, and I wondered how these modes of experience would ever become reconciled. I felt as if I were constantly moving between one dimension and another. It was rather like running up and down stairs the whole time, trying to hear what the Devas had to say. Gradually the Devas helped me to realise that we all coexist as part of the same whole, and that there is never any separation or gap between humanity and Nature. The Devas are present in every place and moment of time. Devic consciousness is therefore constant, part of the reality we share.

My contact with the Devic level of consciousness grew out of a love of and a particular affinity with trees, plants, wildflowers and rocks, and my attunement to the Devas developed naturally from an instinctive response to detail and beauty in the landscape. I have come to know the Devas in simple ways, through observing Nature as closely and in as much detail as possible. As a child I loved to immerse myself in primroses, and I used to bury myself in them so completely that I could feel the very fullness of their presence before me, their delicate fragrance, and soft, pale petals pressed against my face, cool and damp and alive. I immersed myself in Nature in a similar way, and I have always found it completely absorbing and full of endless wonder. A love of Nature continued with me into adulthood, and it is this love of Nature which led me to the Devas.

Because our usual perception of life is largely determined by our physical experience of reality, it can be difficult at first to grasp the infinite levels of consciousness which lie beyond the physical life with which we normally identify. But as soon as we move beyond the finite terms of mental consciousness, we begin to experience and discover how other areas of consciousness are interwoven with the structure and substance of our physical world. We pass beyond what can be known with the physical senses to the subtle world which lies between the mental and supramental levels of consciousness.

The subtle world contains the level of Devic consciousness, the powers of plant and animal life, and the Elemental powers of earth, water, fire and air. These forces of Nature form a completely ordered and integrated whole. It is like a network in which each level has its own sphere of activity and purpose. Together these levels of consciousness envelop all life-forms in Nature, creating the essential patterns which manifest in the physical forms and wonders of the natural world.

The subtle world is perceived with heightened levels of sensitivity and awareness. We move in shifting states of awareness and different registers of experience continually. We do not abandon our physical senses in order to sense the subtle worlds, rather it involves a shifting of sensory wavelengths to a different vibratory level. In fact, the physical senses play a very important part in altering conscious states and drawing our perceptions to higher levels of awareness. This was pointed out to me by the Sweet Pea Deva which flowered very late one summer in the garden. Each time I stepped into the garden I was aware of its delicate

blooms etched with mauve, and the sweet fragrance waft-
ing from where it grew intertwined with the roses by the
cottage windows. It said:

> *We greet you with our softness and our fra-
> grance. We bring forth to you our shining
> qualities, our fragrance and purpose of being! We
> shed forth in abundance, and we bring you to us.
> In appreciation of colour and fragrance,
> humankind perceives qualities which draw us to
> you and you to us. We bring you to the threshold
> of a world of light. Beyond fragrance and colour,
> our purpose evolves and radiates inwards to the
> source of life itself. From this point outwards, a
> movement of light is at work to bring forth from
> within the qualities of life which enrich your
> world. Fragrance and beauty are not insubstan-
> tial, ephemeral qualities but are features of life
> which make their mark in the physical world. Why
> else would we be brought to so many gardens? We
> are as real as the trees and the tinkle of water in
> the stream. We wish you to see the inner pattern
> which rules the outer, and which is the source of
> wonder and diversity. It creates all the beauty
> which stirs your senses and awakens you to our
> world of light, and what we are in essence. Remem-
> ber, all that is given forth to without emerges from
> within, radiating from the centre of light and born
> on a purpose. To be connected with us is to be con-
> nected with the Source, and thus we are joined in
> celebration of the One Light and the Source of all.
> We radiate peace and joy upon you, glad to share
> our gifts with you this way.*

The Devas do not therefore belong to a separate level of reality but surround and envelop the physical attributes of
Nature. They are present in the qualities and characteristics
of plants, such as fragrance and colour, which attract us to
them. When I lean against an oak tree in the wood, and feel

the magnitude of its solid trunk supporting my back, and its roots anchored to the earth beneath my feet, I feel the tree as a living being, with all its strength, maturity and power. It is a feeling of contact with the very essence of the tree as a living organism. It is this sort of contact which brings us to the essence of Nature and gives us our experience of being part of a living world. Thus the Devas draw our attention in a multitude of ways: the texture of frosted leaves; the tall stems of daffodils rustling in springtime; the springy resilience of heather in summer; the gloss of a freshly fallen horse chestnut as it lies in its milky, soft casing. The Devas are present in all these things, for they represent the creative force that brings each of Nature's forms into expression.

Before we even begin to see the plants and wildflowers which the Devas manifest in our gardens and countryside, they are active in every detail of a plant's growth. The Deva of a tulip, for example, brings together all the qualities of energy which determine the development of the tulip — the length of its stem, the shape and texture of its leaves, the colour of its petals and centre, its height and shape, its fragrance, its growing season — its entire development from bulb to mature flower. The Devas ensure that individual plants unfold in absolute perfection, according to their essential pattern of growth. They draw together all the essential energies necessary to create the plant in its physical form. Each species of tree, plant and vegetable therefore has its own Deva, its own conscious stream of life. Time lapse photography, where a film sequence is speeded up, is able to show the development and growth of plants in their true pattern, a continuous flowing movement.

The Devas are part of the angelic hierarchy, and they occupy their own level within this particular field of consciousness. This consciousness is different to that of humanity and is very pure in nature. Because the Devas are responsible for the archetypal patterns within Nature, they bring great balance, order and form to the natural world. Their work is concerned with bringing the life of each species through to perfection, and so this level of consciousness has a particular harmony and resonance. It is this harmony and resonance which we immediately experience when we step into a wild, undisturbed place.

The Devas are aspects of divine consciousness and their existence is unified with the Divine at all levels. They describe themselves as stemming from a central point and divine source which they often refer to as the Centre or the Source. The Devas of my vegetable garden explained their relationship to the Divine as follows:

*We each have our individual role, and we are distinguished by our own unique essence and purpose. It is on this individual level that we work to shape and form, and build the matter of life, to draw essence into being. But the essence is from the collective energy available to all life. You are part of this too. Thus when we say we 'gather' essence, it is a bringing together of the energy available to concentrate our work here. The force we speak of is a great source of light and life-giving energy, given from the Centre. It is an aspect of the divine Oneness — it is the pure love and power of divine Light. It lies in all things and all matter is blessed with this light, and thus we are charged with our own individual tasks and imprints. It is the light source to which we all belong and which causes life to shine and take its creative forms. Together we uplift and aspire — all life is perfected at its own level and what we seek here is to bring this about, in utmost perfection, and to work in accord. Gathering the essence is our foundation work, a preparation so that essence may form more naturally and in unity with all. Thus we seek to harmonise and balance, so that when life enters, it is easy. We are established here, but it is the balance of essence that is crucial. The force is the light of the Great Oneness,*

*God's creative power and our living gift. We add*
*our blessings to all life, and when you come to us,*
*we sound our note in harmony.*

The angelic stream of consciousness contains the Devas of
all species of trees, plants and vegetables as well as the
greater energies of landscapes, and the Elemental powers.
Although the word 'hierarchy' is often used to describe the
different levels within this field of consciousness, it is important to understand that this does not represent a rigid structure of forces and energies. While each level or strand of consciousness comprises different vibrations of energy and life-
force, each has its own unique role and purpose to fulfil and
each contributes to the whole. The entire balance of creation is held together by the interaction between these combined energies.

Initially I was rather confused by the seeming complexity of the Devic realms. I was puzzled by how so much
detail could be woven together. I began to see that it is the
interaction of these energies which is so important, and why
the Devas had emphasised the importance of seeing the connections between living things. It is impossible to look at
any one thing in isolation, because each life-form is innately
connected to everything else. The whole of Nature is a pattern of interacting forces and energies. While the messages
I have received from the Devas of individual species are singular in character, the Devas always place their existence in
the context of a collective energy. I began to see that just as
we are not separate from the Devas, each strand of consciousness in Nature is interconnected. The whole of Devic
consciousness is focused on the work of creating balance,
fulfilling patterns, and adjusting the natural order. Nature is
constantly evolving as a dynamic unity.

So the Devic realms form an interdependent network
of light and energy which is very intricate and unified. The
Devas of individual plants and trees work closely with the
Elemental powers of earth, water, fire and air to bring plant
life through to a physical form. The Cabbage Deva, for example, is dependent upon the earth in which it grows, the qual-

ity of the soil and the levels of moisture and warmth within it, as well as air and sunlight to create the conditions favourable for a seed to germinate and grow. On a much greater scale, whole life systems and ecological zones are formed and balanced by these interacting energies.

One day in high summer, I was walking through sand dunes to a beach on a Hebridean island, and I spotted the most exquisite crimson flower, forming blazing stretches of colour in the machair, the lime-rich shell sand dunes of the north-west Highlands and Islands of Scotland. It grew amidst marram grass and other colonising plants. I was drawn to it immediately. I had not seen this wildflower before and it shone out amongst the grassy dunes. This was the bloody cranesbill flower. It was present amongst other wildflowers growing in the thin, sandy soil: wild thyme, white clover, birdsfoot trefoil, eyebright, selfheal, lady's bedstraw, and daisies, to name a few. I sat for a while studying the bloody cranesbill in detail. I was thrilled to discover this plant and after a while the Bloody Cranesbill Deva came forward and communicated the following:

*I add my own distinctive brilliance to the machair. To this landscape of sand and sea I belong and shine in splendour. I am related to all around, and I take my place as PART of the machair. My gift of life is a contribution, and each life here forms a precious part of the whole. I am come here THROUGH the pattern laid down in the evolving circle of life. We are all weaving and building continually. You must see me in the landscape I belong to, for though my colour is most singular, I speak of the elements and all that is born on the sea wind. And so I am related to sand, air, water — my essence is evolved through the interaction of all parts, and my presence here becomes a flowering gift, no lesser, no greater than the whole — the sum of all parts joined together in harmony, one song sung in unison. See how we all belong here together? It is community and communion, for here we share life and each places its steps within the machair pattern. So it is formed from the combination of these steps, from the tiny to the widespread.*

*Our message is humility and coexistence. For on our own, we form our own unity, but we come through the pattern of life here. Without one, the other would not hold. And so simply, we exist, and what you see is what we bring, offering ourselves to life in great simplicity. No complications, just life itself. Much is contained in this simple act of living — in it lies the divine gift, given to the tiniest element of life; for all life is sacred and all belong. We greet you to our meadow, and wish you well.*

I was very moved and struck by this message. I had been drawn to this plant because of its extraordinary, vibrant colour and here it was pointing out to me that it was part of a community of plants, and that its presence in the machair was due to a combination of forces and life-forms, creating the conditions for life to take hold in the sand dunes. Instead of looking at things in isolation, the Devas encourage me to take a broader look at life, to see how intricately woven life really is. The Devas often point out that our human lives are equally part of Nature and that we are similarly interlinked, not only in the form of human communities and social structures, but within the greater community of all sentient beings.

Through simple, yet profound encounters such as these, the Devas began to expand my view of life. The true value of these communications is that the Devas illuminate the oneness of reality, and the lack of separation at any individual level from the totality. Nature is a cyclical flow of energy from the microscopic to the macrocosmic, and within the perpetual motion of life expanding and contracting, passing from one level of growth to the next, patterns of life are at work, unified by the light of cosmic consciousness. Each life is a gift in relation to the whole, whether in the plant world, or within human society.

The Devas have taught me a profound respect for the unity of life and the uniqueness of its individual forms. Sometimes I have communicated with very small plants, plants which are easily passed by unnoticed, either because they are tiny or because they are very common and we are used to seeing them. I have often been surprised by the tremendous sense of light and power which the tiniest of plants have communicated to me. In spiritual reality, there is no greater or lesser, no "this is more useful than that", no "I like this more than I like that"; for every single aspect of life has its place of belonging and value, and each being is equally blessed and infused with the light of divine consciousness. This the Daisy Deva highlighted for me with great vigour on a grassy bank by a deserted beach on a fine day:

*We greet you! We wish to communicate to you something of the light and radiance of our world. Can you imagine a light so brilliant, that it contains within it whirlpools of radiant colour, more beautiful and subtle than any combination of colours created within the palette of the physical world? Not just gold and silver, colours which denote a certain quality to you, but colours which pulsate within, flowing and molten, like the fluidity of a fire, or the iridescence of a rainbow? We glow with our inner light. This is the essence we shed forth, adding brightness to all things. Colour is an important ASPECT of our light. Within, all is a glorious moving whirl of life. Life is our essence, for this is our being and reason for existence. Therefore when we speak of light, we embody vitality, glory and wonder, contained in the simple fabric of our form — here adding brightness in the simplicity of a grassy bank. But we are LIGHT! We too add our sparkling tones to the vibrancy of this bay — the sparkling sea and golden sands are vibrant with our COMBINED essence. We too take our place here, proudly and in utmost dedication to the light of the Centre. From within to without, the light pours outwards to the simplest, tiniest form. All life shines with its own radiant nature. It is so exquisite, we wish to convey to you the wonder of the inner light, so that you may apprehend this as you walk amongst us. Our light is mingled and part of the shining brilliance of this bay on a summer's morning. Walk amongst us! Know us as we are and step within! Awareness of our light opens the way. Step inside and you will come closer to the perfection and simplicity of the Divine, revealed in true glory. This is our message always, for this is how we serve life. We leave you with our radiant blessings which we shower upon you.*

When I receive messages from the Devas, they are always accompanied by a great sense of welcome and a feeling of moving into a field of energy which is expansive and light-filled. The Devas long to reach human consciousness and for us to experience the true reality of Nature. We have an instinctive, sympathetic bond with the natural world, and the Devas constantly speak of our mutual belonging to the earth. They call us to appreciate the creativity and life which surrounds us, and sustains our very existence. There is a wisdom deep within the essence of the natural world, which has much to teach us about our own patterns of growth, the purpose of human life and our relationship with Nature. The Devas of the mosses, ferns and rocks of a favourite place I have visited since childhood came forward jointly with the following message:

*All surrounds you with the boundless light of our worlds. You have entered our peaceful domain and you are welcome. We beckon you further into our radiating patterns of light and movement, for all scintillates with the pure essence of love, pulsating and radiating in all things. The peace and collective unity you feel in this place IS the pattern which we work to create, for we are life-builders. If only humans could respect this pattern, and know that the peace they sense in wild places were but part of the whole to which they too belong, we could stretch further together in our shared understanding of life. Now it is time to banish separate notions of self. All life is but a shared, intricate dance in which each life-form plays its essential role, embracing the pattern of life by its own evolving essence and part in the great chain of life. For interlinked we are, each woven to each other for our creative benefit and survival. The unity of this chain is essential, and furthers life. What else could have formed the richness of the system which surrounds you here in untouched splendour?*

*We try to communicate to you the essential message of unity for now we enter great times of change and we experience our interconnection most closely. Now is the time for humankind to step forward with us. Never before have the opportunities for expansion of awareness and consciousness come so close. Woven together, we influence creation through mutual recognition of our roles and our work to unfold. Past patterns may be broken, and greater purpose and harmony result. This we desire. This we see in the unfolding story of life. Now is the time for reconciliation with humankind. It must be born out of awareness, mindfulness and true dedication to each life-form. In awareness is born the realisation of our interconnection and divine purpose, In awareness our love for each other and the true meaning of life shines forth.*

*Open your eyes and your hearts, we say! Let life quicken with the true love of all beings and all of living Nature! We are all unified by this love and now we enter it and experience it together. Profound is the opportunity and it is our joy to wit-*

*ness the changes on earth. It is of utmost timeliness and significance for the balance of the whole. In this you play your part. We give praise and sing our joy about you. Love unites all!*

The Devas describe their work as work of light, derived from the central force of divine consciousness. Since they are beings of light, if we were to see them with our physical senses, no doubt we would see them in forms and patterns of light. Some people have this developed visual ability and in traditional societies where an intimate bond with the earth still exists, such ability is commonplace. The Oak Deva spoke to me one day about the particular quality of light in Devic consciousness and how matter is formed from it. The message came on a particularly bright autumn afternoon, from deep within an oak glade in northern Spain. It said:

*We greet you on a day of perfect luminosity! Light is not a physical phenomenon as you would understand it, for though it illuminates all aspects of the human sphere, and what you perceive as physical reality, it is not solid and it cannot be regarded as such. Our light is an essential energy, a shimmering of many particles of essence, dancing and whirling in motion. All is shaped by this whirling light and movement. Life is created in an instant. It is a direct energy, quick and silvery like water, never ceasing to flow. Thus particles are moved and light dances! We are never fixed and static, therefore we remain light in matter. In physical matter we assume greater density for it is required for our materialisation. But the light is not lost, for THROUGH light we shape life, and in this oak wood, layers upon layers of life and light have radiated into form.*

*Is it not a miracle of creation, that light can move from something as exquisite as our light forms, to create the complexity of our trunks, branches, leaves, roots and leaf litter? When you view the physical aspect of a wood, think always to the pattern, the spirit of light that moves creation. Think to our highest point of origin, to know this light and acknowledge its presence in life. In acknowledgement of this light, you acknowledge the divine Source of all. It is not a distant realm, but part of all that surrounds you. All is cast in light and it is beautiful indeed!*

The Devas exist as patterns of light whether we see them or not, but we can become more aware of their presence in Nature. While they exist in their own field of consciousness, the Devas are part of everything which surrounds us and the boundaries which seem to separate us from them can be transcended in a moment. Instead of being partially conscious, we can discover at a fully conscious level our true oneness with the natural world and the exquisite vitality of life in each of Nature's forms. In so doing we can open to the presence of the divine Light in all things.

The Devas remind me continually that there is so much more to life than meets the immediate eye. In the Western world our attitudes are directed towards a material view of reality and a rational understanding of life. There is a need for our culture to expand its focus and move on, to recover elements of the sacred and to view no longer the mystical and the non-physical as a marginal part of human experience. As a child I knew intuitively that the earth was alive and my experiences of Nature and wild places were full of a spontaneity and sense of belonging to the greater living world. Why should we lose this sense of living connection as adults? Is it so unreasonable to communicate with plants if we can experience Nature as alive?

The experience of different levels of consciousness has a profound effect on our vision and understanding of life, but such experiences need to be anchored and grounded in daily life if they are to have meaning and purpose. The Devas wish us to see the intricacy of living systems and to bring a conscious awareness of Nature into greater focus in our lives. The gap that has opened as a result of our mechanistic view of the world has to be bridged. We need not feel the isolation that stems from the withdrawal of spiritual reality from everyday life. There are no barriers which separate us from Nature, for we share consciousness with all living things. When we recognise this essential relationship, then we can begin to see how we can co-operate with Nature. As I walk in the woods, the sight of small flowers dotting the ground, amongst a mosaic of mosses and fallen leaves, reminds me continually of the Devas' message of coexistence and unity. It is right beneath my feet as I walk, in the shifting fabric of the woodland floor. Nature is always changing, life moving in different patterns. When I walk in the woods, I am brought back to the Devas' perspective of life, and the harmony which naturally arises when mental preoccupations subside and a limited sense of self is transcended. I feel the Devas calling me to look at the abundance of creation all around me and to acknowledge the divine presence that is in everything.

The Devas have taught me an integrated view of life by gradually guiding me to see life not in fragmented parts but in terms of the relationships between things. This view of life may seem extremely simple as a concept, yet it is profound, and I continually find new expressions of it in daily life and within the natural world. Each phenomenon in Nature is sustained in a cyclical movement of ebb and flow, of one force acting on another, energy acting on matter, the energy of one element upon another, expansion and contraction, increase and decrease, the rising and falling of vital energy. This continuum is maintained by constant adjustment which the Devas bring through their essential patterns and movements. We may only see the outward forms, but deep within Nature, life arises from the interaction of these mutually dependent forces.

One day I received a very clear symbol during my daily meditation. It emerged with crystal clarity and conveyed the oneness of life which the Devas communicate. The symbol was of a golden web, exquisitely beautiful, and perfectly formed in structure like a spider's web, with radiant strands of golden light and energy. At the centre of the web the golden light formed a brilliant concentration, as if all the strands of the web were illuminated from this central point. I understood that the whole of life is contained in this symbolic web, and that the light illuminating its form represented the pattern of divine Light which embraces the whole of humanity and Nature. The Golden Web is symbolic of the relationships between living beings, and of the true, essential unity and reality of our world.

The Golden Web encapsulates the embracing nature of divine consciousness and the harmony and order of Nature with which life is sustained. The divine Light is everywhere and in all things, and everything is infused with its radiance and power. The centre of the Golden Web, the source of divine love and power, is the source of all life. The divine Light glows at the centre of the web and radiates outwards to sustain and illuminate life in all its forms. In the Golden Web, each strand of life receives this light and sheds it outwards; each fine thread is connected to another; each being and life-form has its place within the interconnected whole. The Golden Web symbolises the divine network of life, of which we as human beings are part, and with which we share our consciousness. It expresses the deep nature of our interconnection with all living things.

In the Golden Web, light is reflected back and forth, as each strand and fibre of light reflects the others. The beauty and light of Nature which we perceive is that to which we also belong, for we are partners of Nature and part of the totality. In the Golden Web, all receive the light equally, and no part is illuminated to the exclusion of another. The network which sustains the web sustains the whole, and each fibre and strand has its part to play; each part exercises an influence and has the potential to experience and affect the other.

The vibrant luminosity and strength of the Golden Web has remained with me as a powerful symbol of life, and I realise that the Devas have been gradually illuminating the presence of the web in all aspects of Nature. It is as if the symbol of the Golden Web has been brought forth through their instruction and guidance to reflect their central message and teachings. Each message that I have received from the Devas has highlighted another aspect of light in Nature and our relationship with it. This is what the Devas mean about the connections between living things. The Golden Web illustrates our true place in the order of things, not as separate egos with a limited, rational consciousness, but as beings engaged in life with a fully developed consciousness of our interconnection with each other and with all beings.

One day in summer, I was sitting in a remote part of the Caledonian forest in the Scottish highlands. I was surrounded by dense mounds of mosses, berries, ferns and lichens carpeting the forest floor underneath the ancient Scots pine trees. Summer sunlight shimmered through the ancient forest, casting pools of colour as the light penetrated the delicate foliage of birch trees. The breeze carried with it the smell of damp, lush growth, and I was aware of the great sense of harmony and mature life within the forest. It filled me with a sense of wonder to think how so much detail could be brought together to create this complete environment. I quietly attuned to the Devas of the forest and the following message came through to describe the weaving of energy in their realms and our part in the divine web of life:

> *This is the infinite spiral of life, for we weave and interconnect continually, forever bringing form and vitality to each plant, species and living thing. It is a continual round — the circle of life to which each form and essence is profoundly connected, and from which it receives its impulse to live, to shine, to grow. Life radiates from the Centre, lives, to return again. We are patterns of light, energy, essence. Our forms and colours draw myriad and minute worlds together. It is the most intricate fabric, so fine it remains imperceptible to human senses, invisible to the unconscious eye. But we ARE here, and permeate life with our*

*whirling pools of soft colour, softness and light,
which swirl and dance to the rhythm of each living being.*

*So it is interwoven and so we unite. What
you see here is the light of harmony, the attunement of Nature to the greater whole. We relate
through the Centre to the Great Oneness. All is
drawn to this power, focus and force, the innate
strength and impulse of life which oversees the
great work of Nature, the large and the small. No
part is greater than the other, for all belong. All
have purpose, form and their own individual,
essential pattern. All belong to the great Centre, the
form of light which shines like a beacon, drawing
into itself and giving of itself.*

*Humanity could learn so much by this way
of being, naturally aligned to the working of love
and light, which so endlessly bestow them with the
essential gifts of life. We say, give of yourselves, your
true, inner selves! Give from that point of beauty
and truth within each one of you, to the greater
benefit of all! You will receive endless joy — thus
inner wisdom unfolds naturally and with grace,
and all unites in the divine pattern and Oneness
of life. All breathes from the same central point. You
are not excluded, or separate from us. You too, take
your part in this light. The light of Nature shines
with richness upon you. Receive, and be joyful!*

*chapter 2*

# Nature Illuminated

Nature surrounds us with its life-giving energies and essential patterns. The Devas are at the heart of this ceaseless activity, drawing and moving light to encompass all that lives and grows. As I walk in Nature and observe the sheer abundance of life and the interwoven intricacies of its forms, I feel irrepressible joy rising inside to see how much life exists and breathes around me in any one moment of time. The further I look, the more there is to see. Each strand of life steps forward to speak of underlying forces at work, moving fragments of beauty into place with mysterious and delicate skill. Each day, new forms are highlighted by changing light and shifts of colour and texture. The vitality and radiance of the natural world resonates from all corners, calling me to witness its revelations, and illuminating details of the Golden Web.

I often find on walks that my attention is suddenly captured by detail. It may be the rich cluster of rowan berries hanging from a gnarled bough; the damp, gritty texture of moss on a glistening rock; the stream of autumn light in billowing grasses under a stormy sky; the delicate traces at the centre of a tiny wildflower; the swollen pearl of a raindrop at the heart of a lupin leaf. For a while, that cluster of berries or the lupin leaf will fill every corner of my awareness as each aspect of it is registered in minute detail. It is this absorption which leads me to a place of quiet, inner focus from which I feel the very essence of the rowan tree, or the lupin, and can hear the Devas speak.

The communications which I receive from the Devas convey detailed information about their level of consciousness and how they weave the web of life. After the Devas have spoken, I feel profoundly connected to all the living forms within the landscape. I no longer feel that I am merely walking through the landscape, for I feel a part of it. The

sense of oneness and belonging is profound and enveloping. The messages convey more than information: they are
encounters with the essence of living things. My interaction
with the Devas involves a flow and exchange, for it is a meeting of consciousness. The Devas exist in all of Nature's forms,
and contact can be made with them at any time. Just as I
turn my attention to the Devas, they turn their attention to
me. The Devas make me aware that I am not merely an
observer in Nature, but that I am part of Nature.

When I first began to receive messages from the
Devas, I was deeply moved by the sense of closeness and
partnership which they expressed to me and which began
to lift me beyond my limited view of the physical world.
There was never any sense that I was excluded from their
way of being and expression. The Devas were overjoyed at
our contact. They long for people to draw closer to them
and to experience the light of Nature and the oneness which
embraces all life. One of the first messages I received came
from the Devas of a remote stretch of moorland by a loch
which I had approached through a wintry expanse of rough
tussock and heather. There was total silence by the loch side,
stirred only by the lapping of water at the edge of the rocky
shore in a gentle, lilting breeze, and the distant chuckling
sounds of grouse in the heather. The Devas of the moor came
forward with the following message:

*We greet you brightly! We offer a quality of light
to all life — brightness in all things! This is
the inseparable nature of the One Source, for life
is born of light and light governs our forms and
activities. We offer you this light at all times. By
appreciating us you share and are part of our
worlds, as we feel closer to you when you tune your
awareness to us. It is a distillation of essence which
is at the source of all life and shines. You can see
this in all life-forms if you attune to it. We have
much to teach you in this sphere. All life is interconnected, and through this process all life shares
and has in common. The light is a creative, loving*

*force — we long to show you the depths of beauty and the boundless nature of life! This is a step forward for mankind. Each time this contact is made, growth and understanding takes place, bringing our worlds closer together, sharing a joy consciously. It releases qualities which cannot prevail if humanity blocks them. It is a time of great rejoicing that our worlds can come close. We thank you and give blessings.*

When I communicate with the Devas, I feel joined with them at their level of consciousness and I experience the immense energy in Nature, unifying seemingly random details. Through the Devas I have sensed the great order, vitality and forces of life at work on the earth, powerfully constructing the living world as we know it. The Devas have also made me aware of the multitude of energies which create the earth's richness and diversity. Powerful movements are at work to form every plant, tree and rock. The Devas describe themselves as builders of essence, gathering essential energies together according to individual pattern. The movement of these energies into place is full of creative impulse and purpose. It is highly concentrated work, for it involves great precision, detail and co-ordination.

First of all the essence, or essential life pattern has to be drawn together. This involves a concentration of light and energy which requires particular focusing. The Devas describe this as a gradual refinement of a defined pattern. It is repeated until specific qualities are combined and harmonised to form an exact concentration. When the essence has been gathered, the blueprint of that species is distilled and crystallised within it. The Hyacinth Deva explained this process as follows:

*We shine and radiate upon you! Essence is formed from a complex pattern of forces and energies drawn together and positioned one to another to form a particular pitch or vibration. It is like the tuning of notes and musical harmonies to form distinct chords. Within these developing patterns, the energies which are brought together influence the overall formation of essence by contributing fine particles of light and energy. The activity which is stimulated by these moving formations is a dance of light and shimmering energy. It is a building of basic life energy. This, as it is building, forms a vibration and wavelength to which the process of life becomes attuned while the journey of growth is assumed. Each pattern that is formed contains unique variations of essence and distinct harmonies of light which characterise the essential imprint of the future form.*

*All is light and moving energy! Our essence is drawn from the energy and light available to all life. It is a moving flow of light which has its source in the divine Oneness. Thus, our beings are formed from the source of consciousness which is shared by all life, and our flowering forms speak of inner perfection and the essential Source of all. The formation of essence depends upon pattern, for we distil only what is needed to fulfil our purpose. Thus we draw to us what is naturally aligned to our vibration and being.*

*It is perhaps difficult for you to conceive how much detail can readily form to manifest in the composite beauty of our forms. Ours is an alignment to ever greater laws of being and patterns of energy. Therefore each draws to its being those elements of light and energy that befit its highest potential for life. We seek no less and thus we work in perfect accord with divine purpose. When you see us, you see us in our resonating and perfected forms. All life is a movement from the inner to the outer. Glad we are to bring the gift of life outwards from the inner source, fulfilling our purpose and singing the glory and wonder of creation!*

The Devic level of consciousness is constantly active and evolving. At no point are the Devas static or bound by the patterns which they create. Their realms consist of constant movement as essence is drawn together and brought into place. The Devas explain that the essence which they use to build life is drawn from the collective source of light and consciousness to which all life belongs, and that it can be drawn in and out of areas in adjustment to prevailing physical conditions. They describe their realms as a fabric of light surrounding all life and which is active at many levels of creation. On an individual level, the Devas fulfil the patterns of growth for individual species, yet collectively they are involved in the whole process of evolution. Nature is continually evolving in movements and shifts which are imperceptible to human senses, but which are nonetheless dynamic and powerful.

Once Devic essence has been gathered together, the pattern or blueprint it contains then becomes fused with life-force and the process of growth and physical formation begins. The Devas hold this essential pattern in place while each stage of growth unfolds. The growing plant is enveloped within the light and energy of Devic essence as the forces of Nature combine to nurture its development. The journey of each plant through to its mature physical form involves an intricate fusion of energies as the basic life-force builds and strengthens to promote growth.

The Devas work at their own conscious level, but they are not separate from the biological processes of life or the physical and climatic conditions which determine growth. The entire process of growth is embraced by Devic consciousness, providing a framework and pattern which binds each stage of development together. Nature is constantly changing and evolving as each strand of life exercises its influence on the creative process.

The Devas remind me that so much more is contained within Nature than we readily acknowledge or perceive and that a great deal of power lies within perfected details of the natural world to make beauty possible. I began to sense that the relationship between essence and form is fundamental to the Devas' work, and so I asked the Iris Deva if it could explain the nature of this relationship. It replied:

*It is a process of becoming — a flowering into a basic pattern which forms a complete whole. All life is guided by these imprints, these subtle maps of consciousness which are the archetypes from which all life is generated. We are the energy and impulse which directs life according to individual specification. Life is ordered in myriad ways invisible to human senses, yet forming a co-ordinated whole. How else could we come through, without the motivation or structure of pattern? All life has its own intelligence and ordering principles. We are the builders which link the threads of life and bind the whole! All form is born from essence, for within essence lie the essential features of form. We contain the entire pattern which generates life through from our level of consciousness into matter. Many forces contribute to make this possible; light, air, moisture, warmth all play their part. All is absorbed and brought in — it is an alignment of energy and life-force to this essential pattern. The building of form is an UNFOLDING and HARMONISING with essence. It is not as haphazard as you would think. We represent knowledge and foresight, for we hold potential and perfection in balance at the centre of our being. Thus when essence is fully gathered, form is a naturally unfolding sequence from within to without. It is a sequence of laws and relationships resonating and taking effect.*

*Do not think of us as bounded by form in a rigid sense, for in so doing you would lose our sense of flowing light and movement. Everything is shaped by the movement of one thing in relation to another. It is a dance of weaving interconnections. We are the steps of the dance, the tune to which all is aligned and co-ordinated. The dance builds and grows, in mounting strength, density and formation. All is born from this essential relationship. The building of life is simply a transformation from one stage of conscious life into the next.*

The relationship of essence and form is therefore one of balance and alignment. Once Devic essence has been formed, each stage of growth becomes a further alignment with Devic essence as physical conditions and biological processes shape the development of the emerging form. It is a sequence of finely interwoven events. The Sea Pink described the intricacy of this process as follows:

*In our essence, we relate to a larger pattern of focus, with which we are in permanent exchange. All life is attuned to this vast wheel of existence, and our being and formation is governed by the greater pattern to which we belong. It is important to understand that our very essence is shaped by that which is greater. Ours is a moving towards our full being, therefore we are ever drawn onwards, like a magnetic energy, in relation to the vibration of energy, force and life-form. If you saw within to our world, you would be amazed by the movement, the activity, the radiance and dynamism of all that moves to shape life. For we are essence builders, and we contain and draw from energy and force to bring forth each species. It is a multiplication of movements and interacting elements.*

*We cannot stress this picture of unity enough to you. You may see us as individual species, which we are, but we are formed through our relationship to that which surrounds us. So we are bridges between land and sea — this is where our pattern slots into the great arena of creation. We glow with the light and energy of the rocks and changing sea forms and patterns! All life has its place within the cosmic unity. You too come to us, with your enquiring and your love of Nature. You too share the same divine love and breath of life which moves and gives inspiration to all. Let us celebrate our oneness! Togetherness is our precious privilege, to recognise each other for what we truly are and to share our awareness of the whole. On this summer's day we shine brightly and radiate our message of love and creativity to reach you and draw you nearer to the heart of essence. It is a work of limitless joy!.*

I am always intrigued by how plants are able to exist and adapt to the most barren and seemingly hostile environments. On a recent visit to the United States, I was fascinated by the extraordinary abundance of life within the desert regions of the Southwest, which in springtime blossom into wild, haphazard gardens, ablaze with flowering cacti and sudden flushes of vivid colour where wildflowers grow in profuse abandon. So much life seemed to be concentrated in this brief flowering season, and within the strange, resilient forms of the desert. Saguaro cacti, the size of trees, tower above the desert floor with limbs like outstretched arms and fleshy, spine-laden stems, and ocatillos explode like giant crimson fountains amidst the desert sage. I longed to understand how such forms of life were able to exist at all, for the desert was a new world for me and seemed full of mystery and inexplicable miracles.

The Pinyon Pine Deva beckoned me to attune my sensitivities to the life of the desert in order to understand its inner rhythms of life. The pinyon pine has a short trunk and spreading crown, and it is able to withstand extreme heat. The tree which spoke to me was growing in the arid crevice of a giant granite boulder. Its compact form seemed to emanate from within the rock, so tightly had the root system become welded to the rock, bound somewhere deep within the very heart of the granite itself. Above the rock, the tree's fragrant boughs stood exposed to the relentless, pressing force of the desert sunshine. I wondered how this remarkable tree could possibly receive enough moisture to grow at all. The Pinyon Pine Deva gave me the following advice:

> *My roots are in the rock, the rock supports my growth, and I am part of it. Great force is transmitted upwards, we are connected. You are surprised at the life in this desert. All the desert is life, evolved over time. The life is ancient and strong. Each bush, each tree has its evolved purpose here — it is more alive than you think! The desert is a powerful form of life, condensed over thousands and thousands of years to its present forms. I am part of it. There is a great energy concentrated here. I would say to you: listen to the air, feel the earth, observe the ground, and the mysteries of the desert will unfold to you and an understanding will come. Go with blessings.*

I followed the tree's advice, and gradually the desert revealed a very different and evolved view of life which began to piece together as I explored its unique forms and wild stretches of temporary blooms. Time and time again the Devas have spoken from the most unexpected corners and from deep within the wildest of landscapes. The messages bring me to a new point of connection and intimacy with wild places. The Devas also vocalise the abundant life-forms to be found in land which humans regard as bleak, barren and void of life. Such areas are often colonised by dense patches of plant life considered of no value to mankind. The vivid flush of rosebay willowherb, thistles, foxgloves and bog cotton are part of our landscape and have their place. Indeed it was the sheer profusion of bog cotton which seized my attention one day as I was walking in the hills. The Bog Cotton Deva urged me to stop and listen, and it came forward with the following vigorous message:

*We greet you, glad that you notice our unique occupation of areas of wild land where little is deemed to grow. But here life abounds! We are most definite, and we create profusion. Profusion is our nature, our purpose IS abundant. Thus banish notions of stagnant bog and see the flowing abundance of life which we create with our billowing silky threads! We love the wind and we love the wet, and we unite all, colonising great stretches with our patient being, cast open to the sky and all weathers. You would not associate patience with plant life? It is a patience of sorts — rather an allowing of life, a making way for life to flourish, and take its part in the truly wild, undisturbed places. Our patience is our willingness to be here, our steadfast purpose in being, and this we are, resolute to reside here, and nod in the wind and the rain, witness of all passing and changing force. Our message is steadfastness and patience, holding the core of life in being and multiplying forth. For we give to our task endlessly, and it is our joy to create form in the simple places. We add our grace with vigour and determination to grow here, and with vigour we say: Courage in being! Sing your song and be proud to bear life! Let the elements play around you, and may YOUR life sing of its own abundance!*

When I hear the Devas speaking to me, I often experience their lightness and fluidity as the messages are transmitted. Yet the Devas are not insubstantial for they conduct tremendous power and energy to earth. I began to understand that all their activity is centred upon an innate sense of purpose, for the Devas represent a pure, unmediated form of energy. I also began to see that their very nature is expansion and growth, and it is the strength and purity of their energy which enables life to be generated so effortlessly.

The Devic level of consciousness resonates with a great richness of light. It is because of the Devas' dazzling concentration of light and vitality that I am often stopped in my tracks to acknowledge some small detail which shines before me, beckoning me to stop and look. The Devas continually enable me to experience Nature in new ways, to honour the miracle of life and the diversity of life-forms with which we share the earth. Beauty encapsulates the light of the Devic realms in endless variations. Each day I am reminded how much beauty exists for us to see and cherish. The Devas show me that the universe is a flowering, breathing whole and that each strand of life within it carries the light and consciousness of the Divine.

An encounter with the Deva of the Giant Sequoia tree brought home to me how much energy and power is anchored in Nature by the Devas, and especially by the Devas of our precious trees. The Giant Sequoia tree is the largest living organism on earth, and the specimen I stood under was a relatively young tree, yet its towering trunk soared above me to a thinning pencil point in the sky way above me. Its majesty of form and immense size was on a different scale to anything that surrounded it in the public garden in which it grew. Its stature and energy was breath-taking, and I felt quite awed as I walked around its gigantic base and gazed up into the canopy. I spent some quiet time with the tree, feeling totally embraced by its vast energy and power. I received the following message:

*I greet you. I am the anchor of the earth. With might and absolute strength I conduct life and force into the earth from the sky. Nothing mediates my growth, for I am absolute. My inner purpose is to reach forward, majestically, in never ending growth, for I simply continue, stronger and ever upwards. Growth is limitless! The whole of Nature is not limited. We simply respond to our pattern, and ever onward we go, in constant formation. You regard us as enormous, but we do not exceed as such, simply expand to fulfil and become. The strength comes from this process of growth, innate in what we are, and how, embrac-*

*ing space and time, we contribute our strength and magnitude to the earth, conducting power from the elements. In our great trunks is stored the essence of time and creation, the many secrets of the forest. Wherever we go, we spread the message of the magnitude of Nature and of the limitless potential of life. It is time to expand boundaries of perception and think through to that which is greater and more abiding. For in our growth, we anchor all that is known in the process of becoming. This we bring to you, and for humankind.*

*Reach high with us — explore ever more into the realms beyond! Feel your feet anchored in the soil and bring your highest aspiration into expression! We watch and guard and store all that is sacred and true within the encompassed core of being, and stand forever with the peace of Nature within us and around us. We speak of this gladly and within us store the imprint of our meeting. This too is drawn into us. Growth is but a constant exchange between all that takes place within an environment, to be given and received in total exchange. Think of all that contributes to the living growth of this moment for you! And so all is united. This moment too becomes stored within as it becomes embedded in the structure of our mutual processes. It is to be wondered upon. Let each moment pulsate with life — give everything to your task and let everything become embedded in the eternity of the moment and in the richness of limitless growth! We leave you in honour and in peace.*

The Giant Sequoia Deva surprised me with the idea that my awareness of it in those few moments could contribute to its growth until I reflected that the Deva was referring to a natural fusion of consciousness that takes place whenever a connection with Nature is made. In those moments of contact we had entered the non-duality in which everything is naturally joined. Whenever we step into Nature and acknowledge each living thing as it truly is, with all mystery and wonder, we can experience the unity which is at the heart of all conscious life. This oneness is present in all things and at all times. It is only the mind that separates in Nature and in ourselves that which is undivided. In the moments I spent with the tree, I experienced its power and vitality as a flow and exchange with which I felt totally connected. Our interaction with Nature is far more significant than we are perhaps aware of. Through a simple manner of being, through awareness of the many living forms which occupy our world, deep connections are made. And so our vitality and consciousness becomes part of all that lives and grows, and we live and grow and are nurtured also.

The Devas, as builders of essence, are concerned with generating life and amassing energy in Nature. This essence and light is not lost when Nature moves into a cycle of shedding and decay. The release of essence which takes place in autumn is vital for all subsequent renewal. When a plant or a tree dies, its decayed physical form returns to the earth where it becomes part of the organic matter which nurtures future life-forms. The life-force of that plant is dispersed with its remains and is absorbed back into the earth. The Devic essence is also released and returns to the collective source of light and consciousness available to all life. In established and undisturbed environments, such as woodlands, rich layers of organic and decomposing matter enable diverse life systems to build and establish themselves.

The essence which the Devas build is not limited by the forms which they create, for the light of the Nature realms resonates and radiates outwards, embracing and bathing all life. It is this illumination which I feel uplifting me as I walk in favourite places and experience within me the vital power of Nature. The illumination of the Golden Web surrounds us everywhere with its fine, shimmering strands of life. The Devas constantly remind me that I also belong to the Golden Web, and that I also am suspended within the living, breathing carpet of life on earth. The Devas make me aware of the embracing power of Nature, the delicacy of its interconnections, and the extreme sensitivity to which all life is attuned.

One of my favourite walks is to a birch wood vibrant with different species of moss and lichen which drape the boughs and the woodland floor. It is like walking into a complete world in which everything seems moulded together in barely distinguishable layers. The birch wood is so undisturbed that when the air is especially still, fine silvery webs interlace the twigs and branches, straddling ferns and fallen boughs, so enhancing the sense of walking into a shining and finely woven tapestry. I walk quietly and lightly, for each footstep has to be carefully placed between deep beds of moss, and I follow thin, meandering pathways formed by the deer. The Devas spoke to me one day about the natural radiance of their consciousness, what this contributes to our physical environment, and how human consciousness similarly resonates and influences the web of life:

*We welcome you to our mossy glade! Here we form a gathered unity and all is brought to a completion. The peace and radiance you sense here is a manifestation of the order we have created, to nurture, balance and refine the essence to an evolved point of unity. This is Nature in its truest form, for we have built and brought growth through each of the evolutionary steps. It is not arbitrary or by coincidence, for great power and force is at work to create what you see here. Now the energy is anchored. Thus a strength and integrity resonates here, which you feel as a sense of mystery and profound stillness. It is our essence, and within lie many completed layers — each worked upon, finely drawn into the pattern, so that each strand is perfected. For perfected we are, and seek no less, and show in our highest form.*

*You in your human world could create what you see here, with the highest part of yourselves. Infinite beauty and creativity abound! Beauty is a result of alignment, when the joy of creation is brought through form. It is a shining of consciousness, the innate light shining through and revealing itself. Drop reticence and come to us in your own fullness of life, form and inner beauty! Shine from within! Bring your qualities forth as we do, to shed forth light to the world and weave and build and further the Oneness of life!*

*We rejoice in creative beauty and to you we gladly sing our song of life. In stillness our sound resounds, deep from the Centre. When you attune to this, your understanding shall deepen, for within the gathered essence lies the fabric of divine life. We wish you peace and we wish you well.*

I have always been fascinated by the unique character of different landscapes and their intimate environments. Often I feel the presence of the Devas in an undisturbed environment very deeply. The Devas explain that they are collectively responsible for the diversity of particular environments and the weaving of life within them. However demanding the environment, the Devas always communicate a powerful sense of belonging and adaptation to the places in which they help to form life. They express a deep sense of connection with the landscapes to which they belong. It was the Rowan Deva which spoke to me one day about the energy of landscapes, and its own particular relationship to mountainous areas:

*I am part of this magnificent landscape and I belong. Belonging is an essential part of Nature's web, as each species and life-form adapts to its own individual character and nature in relation to life around. Place is therefore a crucial aspect, for place is not merely location but shapes the conditions for the retaining and harmonising of life to its source. I am suited to the mountain and here I take my place in the wild spaces of open hill. The bare rock is my environment. This is how it has come to be. Formerly I was part of great wooded stretches, now I tend to grow in isolation. But I am not diminished. My strength lies in my sense of belonging, and I am aligned to these hillsides as the rain is to sky and the stars to the heavens. Our place of belonging is our anchoring point. Each Deva works to bring the pattern through — we are drawn to build and unfold life wherever it is favourable. Our life-producing is endless for we flow according to the laws of our essential nature, moving, ever-building and forming life according to the rhythms of the elements. And so in the wild places, I am a tree of the mountainous areas, and I am aligned to rock and wind which shape my individuality. The mountain is my source and point of reference. We are part of each other. We delight to occupy the high spaces and my song of life pours forth to all that belongs to the mountain and the wild. Belonging is a true connection with the whole and I am part of the mountain. This is my essential character and place of being and I am united with all that lives and breathes here. Blessings.*

The Devas point out that the placement of flowers, for example, is not 'arbitrary' and that their patterns of life are part of a much greater network of energies within Nature which is continually evolving and adjusting. Yet I wondered how the Devas determine location and how they would explain the positioning and inclusion of particular species within a given environment, taking into account soil conditions, available seed sources, moisture, heat, light and so on.

This question resurfaced when one early summer I was delighted to discover that bluebells had colonised an area of the garden beneath a rowan tree. I was overjoyed to see this haze of blue appear beneath the boughs of the tree, and I was strongly aware of their presence in the garden. The Bluebell Deva brought home to me the immense precision of Nature and the tremendous power at work to bring specific forms of life into place. I was astonished by the power and determination which the Bluebell Deva communicated to me. It said:

*I come forward to speak. Our kingdom is related to place. We take our place where the forces are gathered to the right vibrational tone, taking shape and form where space is made for us and we can lay down our pattern. Our pattern is like shades of night sky, swirling, deep and shady. Our kingdom is a field of distilled energy — together we interconnect our imprints and manifest through dense colour. You notice this haze of blue in our glades — heavenly, like the star-lit expanses. We too have our nightly and daily rhythms, and our times of great brilliance. Great movements are at work to bring us here, no lesser than the stars or heavens. We are a concentration of heightened force, and when we occupy a certain site, like this knoll by the rowan tree, it is the culmination of many energies dancing together — working to define a particular field. Thus we sweep in like kings to our appointed place. Nature has its design and knows our coming. We are most specific by nature, specific in our role and destiny.*

*We absorb moon and star energy — strongly we absorb these qualities and anchor them. You too, when you come to us place your garlands of joy and love for this place amongst us and these are drawn into the pattern. Our fruition is proud, grand and timely and we welcome you to our perfumed glades. Come and be still! Be at peace always! Peace is the right alignment of force, the harmonious shining of light through the divine Oneness. Now you will see how we have come! Feel the peace from this divine adjustment. Know that we are joyous and celebrate! Join us in the loving force at the centre of our glade and go with peace of mind.*

The Devas emphasise that their very nature is wholeness,
for however small or tiny the plant, their work involves creating complete, and therefore perfected patterns of life. Each
life-form which they contribute to earth is an expression of
the Divine, a gift of life given to the whole. Their energy is
endlessly productive and giving, constantly affirming their
essential light and creativity. The Devas speak with boundless optimism and joy, for their level of consciousness is pure,
refined and constant, like the uninterrupted flow of clear
water from a spring. Their existence is completely orien-
tated towards creating harmony on earth. It is no wonder
that they have so much joy to communicate to us, for they
have much strength and inspiration to offer humanity. The
Devas long for us to notice the abundance of life which they
shower upon all corners of the earth, in countless unique
forms. One summer, as I walked through a profuse wildflower meadow, the Devas spoke to me of the abundant
stream of life which flows forth into the earth :

> *We greet you once again to our undisturbed
> place, with joy and delight to share our bless-
> ing of life with you! We surround and envelop you
> here with our life-forms. This is our expression of
> life and it is indeed heavenly, for in this peace and
> totality, life is heaven-born, come from the Centre
> with its own message of light, expansion and joy.
> What you see about you is the heightened expres-
> sion of life and unity, for the abundance of life-
> forms speaks of our creativity and the diversity of
> all life within Nature. This is how it should be! Here
> we exist in plenitude and in the full peace of our
> natural rhythms. It is a work of love, united to the
> forces at work upon us, and our own natural pat-
> terns. Nothing in the way, no disturbance or mal-
> treatment. So we pour forth — our gift is life, life,
> all life!*
>
> *In our beings, light is shed forth, undimin-
> ished - our fullness and radiance here creates a
> total pattern and luminosity. What lies here is a*

*precious gift. It is heaven upon earth, life as it should be in perfect balance. Each form takes its place harmoniously, and great force is anchored to the earth. Life is not survival — existence is a GIFT! We have purpose, to live, to build and to grow, and when this is poured through and manifested as we do here, we anchor the gift of our essence in great chains of pattern, inter-being and inter-connection. Thus a fabric of essence is built.*

*This cloth we spread upon the land. It is the cloak, the protection, the joy of creation. It is the distillation of all that grows to move life, to evolve and cloak the earth with life. This we do to great perfection. It is a question of balance and part-nership, allowing life to adjust to the rhythms and conditions which favour life. Here the rhythms are uninterrupted and ancient, but it is not always so. We surround you with our life, our love, and our light. May our peace and harmony continue to inspire you and speak of our worlds. We have much to share and it is our joy to do so.*

The Devic level of consciousness also includes mineral and rock formations. I did not expect to be able to communicate with rocks, but some of my earliest contact with the Devas took place with rocky areas of landscape. Throughout my life I have always enjoyed discovering rocks as much as I have trees, flowers, fungi, birds, insects and wild animals. As a child I gathered stones as special treasures: the silvery glitter within pieces of coarse granite; the sea-washed jewels of rocky shorelines, smooth to touch and hold in the palm of the hand. I gave names to individual rocks in the landscape and I spent hours clambering upstream following favourite routes marked by selected boulders. Rocks were also special vantage points, from which I could view the secrets of the natural world. One day, while sitting peacefully on a favourite boulder anchored midstream in a river, the rock communicated its powerful presence and strength in the following message:

*My essential properties are of unique origin, and through me shines the light of many gathered light beings which form my solid matter. Here I occupy this central position in the burn, and I am glad, for I rejoice in my partnership with the forces of earth, air and water, today warmed by fiery sunshine which casts all in glowing warmth and radiance. In my stillness and solidity lie great wisdom and profound resources. It is an anchoring of great power, and so you were drawn to this anchor point in the burn. We shape and blend our qualities in the ceaseless motion and creation of life, and our gift to life is our stored qualities. Thus I seem unchanging, but I am alive! I breathe unity, oneness and creation, and my stored force and essence adds strength to this intimate landscape. Within, all is light and brightness. You would be surprised if you could see the dazzling glow of my inner essence — a scintillating pattern of colours and light unimaginable. Rejoice in our contact! I welcome you to my domain. May we jointly send out our love to all creation — you in your way and I in mine. I rejoice in this understanding. Great is the glory of life!*

The Devas have shown me that everything in Nature is alive and has consciousness, and that as human beings we are part of Nature and a greater flow of conscious life. The Devas point out that we occupy a position in the Golden Web which influences the balance of life as a whole. The power of human thought and activity has its own contribution to make to the well-being of life on earth. We each have our purpose of being and we all belong together. Each strand of consciousness in the Golden Web has its own value and contribution to make.

The Devic level of consciousness also includes the great Elemental forces of energy which are active in earth, water, fire and air. Like the Devas, the Elementals are dynamic forms of light and energy which exist in their own life-stream, and they have their own level of conscious activity. They govern the movement and formation of the elements, and therefore they are constantly active in shaping conditions on earth. I have experienced them as a raw, motivating power, a vast, dynamic strength within Nature. The Elemental powers encompass a great range of activities and manifestations, helping to form the substance and evolving order of the earth.

We easily recognise the power of the elements in their many different physical guises: the thundering curtain-like torrent of waterfalls; the majestic outline of great mountains; the warming power of radiant light as the sun lifts from the horizon and brings a new day; and the wild, cleansing energy of wind. We also respect the awesome effect of their power in earthquakes, floods, hurricanes and volcanic eruptions. The Elementals shape the forces which constantly transform and restructure life on earth as we know it. They are responsible for the whole creative order within Nature, the changing movements which regulate Nature's rhythms and cycles.

The Elemental level of consciousness not only shapes the elements which bring balance and structure to the earth through their respective phenomenal manifestations, but they also influence life at many subtle levels. One day, when I was sitting by the stillness of a Scottish loch, the Elemental power of water reminded me that even at the heart of stillness, a particular quality of energy is generated which is capable of transforming our conscious state, and calming our physical energies. The message I received reminded me of our constantly shifting levels of awareness, the great fluidity of our energy, and our innate sensitivity to the rhythms of Nature's vital forces. The flat calm of the water mirrored every detail of the surrounding hillsides, the trees, the heather, the clouds and the sky. The message said:

*In stillness, all is concentrated and becomes clear. All moves to a point of tranquillity from which balance and harmony may be absorbed. You reach us in this tranquillity, and in these moments all life is open. Contact is made more readily. It is like an attunement to the greater overall unity. We stress to you continually that all is unified, for without this basic harmony which binds all life with a common purpose, life could not be sustained. And therefore stillness is a point of balance, a point of reunification, when that unity becomes more apparent. Consciousness opens and deepens and the path to the true divinity within all life becomes clear — a greater perception is given. This is the true reality. This remains the same whether you are tranquil or not — it is there, only if it is realised by the awakening within you. So, be at peace, and listen to the inner heart of stillness which beckons you through to our realms. The reflection is a mirror of all life. Thus all gathers light inwards to reflect back, and to shine from within. You do this too. You are capable always of this stillness and peace of mind. Come to us! Feel with us the total stillness and energy gathered in these moments of light and great shining glory! Let Nature carry you into the shining perfection of our inner worlds, that you may know yours! We radiate life upon you!*

Everything in Nature is structured through a ceaseless flow of energy, and through the many levels of consciousness which weave and thread different forms of life together to form a changing and dynamic whole. This movement and dynamism is reflected throughout Nature in its changing rhythms, the cyclical passage of the seasons, the movements of energy which shape individual forms and the cohesion of life which creates unique ecosystems — all is shaped by these constantly evolving patterns, by the relationships that exist within them, and the forces of life which bring them into place.

     The patterns of seasonal change are crucial to the regulation and balance of life on earth. The Devas' activities are attuned to these essential laws of change like a pulse of life. It is this harmonious order within Nature which I love to experience in the familiar, repeated signs of the advancing seasons: the protruding spears of daffodil stalks within the grass; the rising fragrance of the warm earth following the first summer shower; the tension of a still autumn day as the first leaves spiral to earth; the frosted patterns of leaves in winter. As the seasons change, the Devas simply move through different stages of activity. We perhaps associate activity in Nature more with the tangible displays of spring and summer, yet the Devas are active even within the encroaching darkness and cold of winter, when life regenerates and essential energies are stored.

The Devas remind me that Nature is full of wisdom and purpose and that they exist to fulfil a harmonious pattern on earth, bringing Nature's cycles to fruition. In their work the unfolding miracle of life is contained in one flowering form after another. The Devas wish us to value and pay more attention to the sensitivity of the web of life and the balance of energies within it. Nature has many vital powers, but they exist as a delicate balance of reflecting relationships which influences all forms of life. The Devas continually refer to the interwoven nature of their realms and the effect of each life on another.   The Devas perceive life with a directness and simplicity which is deeply refreshing and uncomplicated. Growth is regarded as an alignment of energies and a natural adjustment to conditions on earth. However brief the flowering season, it is never insignificant, for it is fulfilled with individual purpose, contributing energy and life on behalf of the whole. This spontaneity and dedication was for me encapsulated by the transient carpets of Mexican poppies growing in secluded pockets of the Sonoran desert in Arizona. I suddenly encountered these vivid displays of rich orange, cup-like flowers where they soaked up the desert sunlight in fluttering swathes of saturated, golden light. The Mexican Poppy Deva communicated its pure joy of being to me in the following message:

*This is our time. Born of rain, we shower the desert floor with our growing, reaching to the sun, formed by the sunlight and the soil. Though*

*our stay is brief, we contribute to the rich diver-
sity of the desert, taking part in the great overall
unity. We give life, for we glow with the light of
desert sunshine. Were you not dazzled by our
colour? Colour is formed, a pattern woven into the
essence of our being. Our world is fused with a
golden light, enabling us to open to the sunshine
and fill our beings. We are formed by the sun and
give through the sun. The air, the soil, and desert
floor are all one. We dance with light in our beings!
There is much joy in our fruition. Gladly we take
our gentle part in the Great Oneness! You humans
would do well to learn the quality of opening with
joy which is our natural state — come to the centre and feel the resonance with which we work !
We are the song of the desert! In joy we attune to
the whole. We contribute to the ongoing fabric of
the desert, and our note lingers after the sun has
gone. Opening and closing is our way. Rhythm and
light is our tune. Linger with us and hear our song!
We are glad you have come to listen and learn. We
bless you with our golden light. Go with joy!*

I have always been struck by the Devas' sense of purpose
and their positive attitude to life. When they compare their
consciousness to ours, they do so in order to encourage us
to develop our own potential for growth, and to remind us
that human life also embraces purpose. They point out that
if we are to understand that consciousness in Nature aspires
to creating wholeness, we should equally accept the potential for creating wholeness within ourselves. Human creativity is capable of endless enrichment and transformation
if we learn to use our higher sensitivities and apply them
wisely. The Devas' direct grasp of life shows me that there is
nothing to hold us back from a deeper consciousness of
Nature, and greater co-operation with Nature in the future.

Often when the Devas communicate to me the quality of light which enriches their world, and their unlimited

energy for creative activity, they also comment on the gifts of human life. These exchanges have led me to think more deeply about the nature of human consciousness. The Devas experience growth as a limitless activity, for they are constantly evolving and renewing life. They see that we are capable of developing our consciousness infinitely beyond the levels to which we are accustomed. The Devas are constantly calling us to expand and awaken, not only to the life within Nature, but also within ourselves.

The Devas each have their own particular pattern of life, yet collectively they strive to bring balance and unity to earth. Aspiration and expansiveness are part of their very nature. The Devas wonder why we have such a limited sense of self, when we are capable of so much creative thought, sensitive awareness and expression. The Devas have a very positive sense of our potential for growth, and the contribution we can make to the world through our individual lives. Nature touches our lives deeply and is a powerful, harmonising and healing force. Through Nature, we experience greater peace of mind and heart, our sensitivity is awakened to other forms of life which have their place in our world, and our vision of life is widened.

The Devas' messages emphasise time and time again the universal responsibility we share to help protect Nature and preserve the future of life on earth. Ultimately the call to act has to come from within, from the human heart and the inspiration of clear awareness. From this place within, we unfold in our journey of life, to develop as human beings and to learn to use our individual gifts. The Cornflower Deva spoke to the heart of humanity in the following message, calling us to embrace purpose and fulfil our highest potential as human beings, thereby honouring our position and shared partnership within the Golden Web:

*We would like to speak. Our world is formed from wholeness, for we are brought to a state of perfection before we are able to unfold our essence. All is created in perfection, and that perfection arises from inner wholeness. This means we transcend and aspire to become, and develop our true nature. It is like a blending and weaving of essences — like growing towards something. As our energy infuses our potential for being, we expand with ever greater force and life radiating from the Centre. Thus like stars we crown our life with delicate hues and patterns. All is part of life's rich unfolding pattern. We know our way and entrust with our beings — manifesting our inner wisdom.*

*Creation involves a knowing of purpose, an ability to shed forth energy to the right pitch and wavelength. We wish you would trust YOUR inner pattern, for the forces which we speak of are not separate to human consciousness. As you reach inward to unfold your true inner self, you will find much innate force and wisdom readily gathered to bring you forward to life. All is purposefully formed to a wholeness. You see life as fragmented parts, but it is not so in our realms. If you were to seek the deeper nature of living things, you would understand the deep inner rhythms which generate and enhance life. We embrace ours, and attune to become completely.*

*Each life has this potential. It lies within you too to acknowledge and aspire to these levels. Each step you take to perceive beauty and wholeness in life around you will bring you to a greater awareness of your own inner richness. For what lies within all living things also dwells in human life, the beauty of the soul to be brought out and defined in the living of individual life. Hear the call! Be prepared to go deep, to a world of inner light and beauty! These dimensions are there to manifest the glory of life. Our shades of blue sing the song of radiant life. Once we grew as wildflowers, and now we are chosen by man to add grace to his gardens. We are glad to come with this message, for ours is a reverence for pattern. The inner order is rich in beauty and form. We share gladly and shower our essence upon you with joy! All life is sacred and when you touch this quality you become part of the sacred dance of life with us.*

*chapter 3*

# Communicating with Devas

The Devas stress that we all share consciousness with Nature, that we are all part of Nature, and that there is no separation between human life and that of the Nature realms. We are all therefore capable of increasing our sensitivity and awareness of Nature. Becoming aware of the consciousness within Nature means expanding our view of life, and it should not be regarded as insignificant. All development of sensitivity is a step forward on the spiritual path and in itself changes consciousness. It enriches all aspects of life experience, as we come to see the total reality of our world, the pattern of our individual journeys and the relationships that are formed. It is a journey which takes us into the heart of life itself.

In my own experience, communication with the Devas developed out of a great love of Nature. It took place for a specific purpose: to bring through an understanding of the conscious life within Nature so that we may begin to restore our relationship with Nature, as we evolve into a new era of consciousness. Throughout my life I have always felt a close affinity with the natural world, and this has been an essential link in my work and experiences. I did not know in advance that a psychic opening would develop in my life. It unfolded as a gift to be used, and grew out of a longing to understand what lies beyond the physical world. Each step was linked to this development and was valuable in its own way.

My journey into Nature began in early childhood. As a child, my sensitivities were awakened through contact with the natural world. I felt most alive and fully attuned when in wild places. There was a presence in Nature, something which called me like a voice to explore everything in detail, and to watch the living world very carefully. My sensitivity attuned to this attentively and longingly, looking for answers.

My love of Nature began at an early age, for each summer my family made a pilgrimage from the smog and grime of city life to a remote cottage in the Scottish highlands. My earliest memories are filled with the excitement of re-entering this mountainous country, with the familiar, towering shapes of the hills, the roaring sound of the burns in spate, the smell of heather, moss and burning peat fires, the veils of mist and cloud rolling in from the sea, and the sound of the wind rattling the roof and gable ends of the house.

Stepping into this wild and beautiful landscape was an immersion into a reality in which each detail became etched in my mind. I had names for rocks and sheltered caves on the hillsides and for each waterfall pool on the burn. As a child I was receptive to the wildflowers and the vivid splashes of corn marigolds in the hayfields, and the flow of clear, peaty water into secret pools shaded by rowan, birch, alder and oak. At night I would prop open the skylight window in my bedroom and watch for the rhythmical flashes of lighthouses on distant peninsulas, drinking in the night air. I loved to study the magical patterns of the stars, and the silvery, liquid pathways of moonlight reflected on the sea. I longed to walk into all this completely.

One day, when I was six or seven years old, I scrambled down a gully to reach a special place in the burn with cascading waterfalls overhung with ferns and honeysuckle. It was secluded and I was aware of the great adventure of walking into such a place alone. Summer light filtered through the oak trees, and the smell of mosses, water and wildflowers swept over me with a soothing and delicious sense of delight. I stood, mesmerised, and drank it all in. The place was bathed in a soft luminosity and resonated in perfect harmony. There was a great sense of peace and calm, and everything seemed connected and at one. All was touched by this gentle light and shone with great beauty.

I cannot recall how long I stood rooted to the spot, for it felt timeless. I remember thinking that this must be what heaven is like. I felt a total sense of belonging and an all-enveloping radiance and joy. After a while, things quietly reverted back to normal, just as they had been before. I remember the indescribable feeling of elation as I scrambled out of the gully in a state of breathless excitement.

I felt as if something very magical had been revealed to me. At some level I knew that the sense of oneness I had experienced was very important, and somehow central to life. The veil had been momentarily pulled back in order for me to see. I remembered this experience throughout my childhood. It remained tantalisingly beyond everyday reality, but I always knew it was there.

Contact with Nature continued to be very important to me throughout my childhood. I spent a lot of time in trees, watching everything moving about me. Hedgerows were the home of primroses and violets, waterfalls the playground of otters, and the early morning before dawn was the hour of the returning fox. My delight was to discover all these things, and to sit quietly and watch Nature at work as she beckoned me further into a world of secrets.

These early experiences with the elements and the natural world were formative, and charged with vitality, wonder and joy. The peace and inner harmony I experienced in Nature were a great resource to me in the years of turmoil whilst growing up, and never lost their force or wonder. I developed a deep appreciation of wild and beautiful landscapes, and I found that my understanding of life was somehow supported by the rhythms and purity of Nature.

When I walked in Nature, I discovered a peace and perspective on life that reminded me of the significance of my childhood experience, and of the oneness which I knew to be at the heart of life. The beauty and detail of Nature affirmed it constantly. It was always in Nature that I found true inner peace, and I sensed the mystery of life lay within its patterns and forces.

As a university student I lived in a cottage close to the sea. Walks by the shore with my elderly neighbour gathering driftwood, the pounding of the winter storms, the subtle changes of light and colour on the sea, the call of oystercatchers and the smell of kelp were all things which I loved and which became interwoven with my student life. As an undergraduate, I began to explore key areas of study which were to have a major influence on my life.

As part of my undergraduate degree in Hispanic languages, I had the opportunity to work in the Peruvian Andes, where I studied the medicinal plants used by the Quechua people. Their medicine not only involved extensive knowledge of curative plants, but also a sacred relationship with the earth and a reverence for the natural world which supported them. This opened the doorway to a very different world-view and a key phase of exploration and study.

Two years later, in 1984, I returned to the Andes to make a study collection of medicinal plants in Bolivia. This postgraduate research focused on the symbolic use of plants in ritual by the Quechua and Aymara communities. My awareness was opened to deeper levels of healing and dimensions of consciousness through the study of shamanistic practices. I was fascinated by how plants and symbols were used to make meaningful ritual patterns which created access to Nature's healing forces.

The rituals and ceremonies which I witnessed expressed a great reverence for Nature. They reflected a rhythmic way of life and thought, and close relationship with the earth. The rituals were intimate gestures of communication, charged with vitality and meaning, and were designed to create an essential balance in life. Their main purpose was to sustain the essence and vitality of the earth in co-operation with Pachamama, or Mother Earth.

The Aymara and Quechua showed me that there were pathways into other levels of consciousness and that communication could take place. All their rituals and customs acknowledged the spirit realms as an essential dimension of life, and I was very moved by the way in which they embraced this much deeper and interconnected vision of reality. At the heart of their healing rituals lay an understanding of the essential balance and harmony within Nature, and the importance of the relationship between all forms of life.

In 1986, while completing my doctoral thesis, I began a three year course in traditional Chinese acupuncture. This involved a rigorous training in sensitivity to ch'i, the energy, or life-force which is observed and regulated in the practice of acupuncture. It involved detailed study of the flow of vitality in both human life and within Nature. The specific laws of healing employed in acupuncture, which is a highly effective and powerful system of medicine, are drawn from ancient Chinese observations of the movements and patterns within Nature. My work with acupuncture gave me a deep appreciation for the uniqueness of individuals and our healing connection with Nature.

The development of the physical senses is an important part of traditional Chinese diagnosis, and the ability to perceive the condition and flow of ch'i involves seeing, hearing, feeling and smelling. Training not only involves the refining of sensitivity to the signs of energy imbalance within patients, but also learning to observe and understand the spirit of the elements, and the cyclical flow of vital energy throughout Nature. This is in addition to the detailed study of anatomy, physiology and the biology of disease. The development of this sensitivity and philosophy of life has been a foundation for all my subsequent learning.

The study of acupuncture taught me not just to understand energy, or ch'i, as a concept, but to observe it at work in Nature, shaping each individual plant, leaf and flower. Just as we learned to trace the energy pathways in the human body through our fingertips, we also learned to use every aspect of our physical senses to feel the energy of the elements, the seasons and their corresponding influences. Learning about the life-force at work within these natural rhythms brought an appreciation of the great order, harmony and vital power of Nature.

This period of training stimulated endless interest in the nature of life and the human condition. It made absolute sense to me that the whole of life is underpinned by vital forces of energy at work in Nature and in ourselves. It fascinated me to discover, within the precise laws of acupuncture, how our relationship with Nature is so intimately connected with the healing process, and why it is so vital for restoring our sense of wholeness.

In 1991, at the age of thirty, my life went through a period of change and I stopped practising acupuncture. I had been involved in intensive study, training and practice throughout my twenties, and it felt important at this stage to have a rest period and review. I sensed that new developments lay ahead and I valued the opportunity to spend more time immersed in Nature, and to reflect on my studies and experiences.

During the following winter, I married my husband, Simon, in the Himalayan region of Ladakh in the far north of India. We had first met in the Andes during my fieldwork. When I returned from Bolivia, Simon and I were inseparable and our journey has evolved side by side ever since. We celebrated our marriage with Ladakhi friends in the deep peace of winter. Snowy mountain peaks surrounded the capital, Leh, like crystals. Everywhere lines of Buddhist prayer flags fluttered on the hillsides in the bright winter sunshine, casting their messages and blessings over the Indus valley.

It was following this visit to India that an opening of psychic sensitivity took place and I experienced contact with the Devic level of consciousness. I was aware that I had psychic ability, and that it was part of my sensitivity to places, people and events. Contact with the Devic level of consciousness was a development which arose unexpectedly in my life, and was to bring with it a wholly new perception of Nature and our relationship with it. It unfolded gently and gradually, and I treated my first experiences cautiously and with great respect.

I had read of Dorothy Maclean's pioneering work with the Devas in the garden at the Findhorn Foundation Community in Scotland, and I had always been fascinated by how her relationship with the Devas had developed into the practical work of co-operation in the garden. Because of the close relationship with Nature which I had observed in traditional Andean communities and my experiences with energy in acupuncture, it made absolute sense to me that one could attune to the spirit and essence of Nature and experience contact. So I had no difficulty accepting the reality of Devic consciousness, but I never thought it was something I would experience myself. With hindsight I realised that this was a completely natural development, and grew out of a readiness to experience these things.

The first time I received a message from a Deva was a very distinct experience. The message was dropped into the pool of my awareness like a crystal clear droplet of rain. It was so lucid, and so penetratingly clear, that every detail of this event remains etched in my memory, still retaining its charge and impact. It was an absolutely specific event, and I had never experienced anything like it before. I immediately recognised that something had happened which was beyond my usual state of consciousness.

When it happened, I was lying on a flat rock close to the sea. My mind was empty of thought and followed the rhythm of pounding waves on the shore. Gradually my eyes fell upon the tumble of smooth rocks at the tide line of the beach, and to my intense surprise, the following message began to be imprinted in my consciousness. It took the form of words, which came in a connected stream, like a typescript flashing up in my mind, and as clearly as if someone was speaking to me, except that the communication was silent. The message was completely disconnected from my own thoughts and came from some other place. I was profoundly astonished. I realised that something extraordinary was happening, but allowed the flow to continue until it abruptly finished. What I heard came from the beautiful rounded stones forming the boulder beach and took the following form:

*We beckon you to become as One with us. We gather here in great stillness and beauty. We radiate and oversee the unity of form. Unity is a drawing up of essential qualities, our formation is a process. Much time is needed to create what you see here. But we are glad you notice. We are timeless and shifting — rhythmically moved by the sea and tide. Thus our essential patterns are united and at one with the forces and shifting sands and water. All is connected. Light and air take their part in our formation, just as matter and substance do.*

*If you saw the shining of our inner forms you would no longer view us as dense matter. All is at One with the great Light and Plan. Feel our smoothness and connect with the whole! We are old and living. Our qualities are anchored here and you perceive our part in this bay. Wake up we say! Gladden in heart and take note of all around you! Great is our wish to be attuned and to reach the corners of your consciousness and unite in joy! All is joy! Be at One.*

My awareness was jolted open by the unexpected happening of this event. The message had come with such a sense of joy and tranquillity, that I was delighted, awed and filled with excitement all at the same time. A distinct peace and calm followed the message, similar to that which I had experienced by the waterfall pool as a child. I understood that the message had come from Nature and had somehow been transmitted to me. I was momentarily stunned, and aware of feeling unusually uplifted.

I walked back along the beach, turning over what had happened in my mind. A great stillness hung in the bay, and for a while I absorbed each detail of the sand, the rippling waves and the rocks which had spoken. Nothing in the landscape around me had changed. Oystercatchers were still calling to each other as they fed in the shallows, the sunshine glistened on a calm sea and the wind gently ruffled the heather by the shore. Everything felt gathered together in the peaceful tranquillity of this wild place, and the unity which the rocks had communicated seemed perfectly reflected in the landscape around me.

I realised that this experience had been an opening of consciousness, yet my feeling of astonishment lasted for some time. I was not so much surprised by what the message contained, but by the fact that this had happened at all. It was a stream of consciousness different to anything I had ever experienced before, and I was not quite sure how such levels of reality could be so suddenly revealed. I thought it over again and again, for the experience raised all sorts of questions and possibilities. Would it happen again, and when and where? Was it normal to experience such things? Why had it happened to me and what would it further reveal? I knew with absolute certainty that I had not imagined it and therefore I could not simply dismiss it. I sensed that a doorway had opened in my life, and that if it had happened for a purpose, all would become clear in time. From then on I always carried a notebook and pen with me, although it was some time before I received another message.

It was important to accept what had happened and to understand why. Having passed through this doorway, there was no going back. My walks in Nature were now filled with a new sense of exploration and I observed everything around me with new eyes. I felt a similar experience could reoccur at any time, and there was a strange expectancy. This period in my life was a subtle, opening process, accompanied by a heightened sense of awareness. Over the following months, further messages occurred, and it became clear that I was receiving communications from the Devic level of consciousness within Nature. The Devas of different individual species began to identify themselves to me. I felt as if fragments of a much greater reality were being revealed to me, to guide me gently forward and to increase my understanding of the intricacy, purpose and pattern of the Divine.

The Devas spoke to me when my mind was perfectly clear and when I was sitting quietly in an undisturbed place. Initially, the messages occurred quite spontaneously and not necessarily when I was expecting them. I gradually became accustomed to the pattern of contact and the nature of these communications. The messages had a distinctive quality which I immediately recognised, and they were always accompanied by a feeling of joy and upliftment which altered my awareness for some time afterwards.

I began to receive messages from the Devas of trees and wild plants. Sometimes the Devas of part of a landscape would speak collectively. Contact with the Devas was not arbitrary, because the messages always occurred when I had become aware of the individual character of a tree, or the details within a landscape. It seemed that the Devas spoke to me as a result of me peacefully absorbing the essential nature of these things and being inwardly attuned to them. I soon learnt that a concentrated focus of awareness was an important means of reaching through to the Devic level of consciousness and that the messages came through when I was in a receptive state.

As these wonderful communications continued, I felt that a relationship with the Devas was beginning to form, and that with each message, I was being encouraged to look at Nature more deeply. The messages were expressed with such loving intention and lightness of spirit, that I felt as if I was being enabled to directly experience the light and energy of Devic consciousness. These quiet and gentle experiences brought with them an increasing sense of wonder. Even when I was not receiving messages, I found that I was looking at trees and plants and stones in a new way, with increased sensitivity to their beauty and individuality.

Up until this time, the messages had come through occasionally and spontaneously, and I questioned whether there were ways in which I could communicate with the Devas, as well as their being able to communicate with me. I was not altogether sure whether it was possible to reach through to their level of consciousness when I chose to. In quiet moments, with my mind absolutely clear of thought, I would sit with a tree, or wildflower and focus my attention on its very essence and detail. Each time, a message came through in a terrific burst of energy, and with a wholly individual character. I also began to ask the Devas specific questions, and this stimulated a great flow of contact with them. It was a great joy to discover that a two-way process of communication was possible, and from then on communication with the Devas has involved an ongoing dialogue which can be resumed at any time.

Initially it was easier to attune to the Devas when I was in a wild place, with my mind clear. Contact with the Devas is always clearly defined, and I know exactly when a message is beginning and ending. All mental activity is stilled. The messages come in a flow of energy which is concentrated, pure and intense. My mind simply serves as a clear, open vehicle to receive the Devas' communications in word form. The Devas' messages are always accompanied by a feeling of energy and lightness, which has become characteristic of our contact. The energy feels soft, light, pure, and swift.

The fluency of the messages increased as I adjusted to the energy with which they were received. Initially I felt stretched to receive this energy and the rapid flow of the messages. In the early days, some of the messages contained pauses while more complex concepts were presented to me. I often receive images which help to illustrate concepts which are difficult to translate into words. The images are symbolic and involve patterns of light and colour which reflect different dimensions. The messages always come rapidly, in a continuous burst, before abruptly finishing. I have found that attunement to the Devic level of consciousness requires perfect inner stillness and clarity of mind.

It was clear from the beginning that sensitivity, coupled with clarity of mind and purity of intention, were essential factors in being able to communicate with the Devas. Clarity of mind was essential for establishing a channel, and intention played an important part in the level of contact. Communication with the Devas involves receiving a very pure quality of energy, and I have always treated these communications with great respect. I sensed that there was a purpose for these communications, and I felt a responsibility to develop my sensitivity in the right way.

I was careful not to contact the Devas if I was feeling at all upset, or unable to concentrate, and I soon learnt to step in and out of a receptive state. This felt like a strange and bumpy transition which gradually became easier with time. Communicating with Devic consciousness involves a certain discipline, like becoming used to a regular pattern and technique of meditation. I also developed ways of remaining centred and protecting my sensitivity at all times. I found that this gradually developed into a pattern of contact which takes place in an atmosphere of great concentration and tranquillity. As I grew more used to our contact, it came more swiftly and easily.

The Devas show me endless patience, compassion and love, and they continually encourage me to see the creative force of love in their work. I often wondered how our contact was possible, and one day I decided to ask the Devas how they perceived the process of communication. They replied:

> *You tune yourself to us, reaching to our world is an act of will. This opens consciousness. You seek us, and when an opening is made, we can make our impressions. We send them as thoughts, but much depends on your receptivity. It is like a meeting, a fusing of consciousness. It is natural, for life IS! You have always seen us clearly, but we could not speak until your consciousness was ready. But it does not mean that contact cannot take place. Love for a place, love of Nature is enough. Many people know and perceive our works and we are grateful. But it is more specific to communicate our world to one who is attuned to the right level. When your heart and mind are attuned to the whole, then there is a readiness, a focusing of energy.*

> *Be not afraid of the power! It is just a heightening of thought. We do our best to shape thoughts in a way you will understand. Thus we communicate in a language which will have meaning. But we use your mind for this facility. You will find the stillness and ability to receive comes more easily as you get used to it. It is a great step forward. We cannot emphasise this enough. Look, receive,*

*acknowledge! Much understanding and growth
will come. Learn to receive your gift. It is a joy for
us and we delight in the level of consciousness we
share. Be glad! All is as it should be.*

One day I was walking along the shoreline of a remote Scottish island and I cut across inland through a wildflower meadow. The flowers formed a thick, nodding carpet around my legs as I walked. I was moved to see such a profusion of life in this undisturbed place, and I felt compelled to sit amongst the flowers and be with them. I had only recently begun to communicate with the Devas, and I inwardly expressed my gratitude for the abundance of life around me. The Devas' response was vigorous, and to my delight a message followed:

*Be not afraid to listen to us! It is but a step
further than feeling a sense of peace here, for we
ARE here, and we have our own voice, our individual purpose. We are numerous here, largely
because we are undisturbed. You see before you an
abundance of life, which is our natural state of
being. We emphasise again and again that our
work is a moving of light. By this you could say a
pulsating force given from the Centre which is able
to take form as it is sent out, like the energy of
sound which carries recognisable characteristics
which you are then able to identify.*

*This is our way. It is movement of life,
rhythm: it is energy, sound, all these things in
essence, and we are the builders. We help individually to work this energy to the correct pitch and
tune, so that like a sound, it can be sent out in its
individual character. Each plant is a wholeness, a
completion, a being of essence formed from light
and born of the One Source. This is a state of natural BALANCE. We hold the threads and rhythms
of life and here we are able to perform our work
with great clarity and ease. Thus the energy builds*

*and grows, allowing life to multiply.*

*Think of the enormous creative potential if man learnt to work with us! Much could come of a creative partnership, a creativity which would match the beauty of these wild, undisturbed places, verdant with life. While this is our natural state, we are capable of all this in YOUR sphere. We long to teach man how to retune to this balance. Where purpose is connected to the right alignment of force, creative power flows easily. We ask you to observe and learn from this.*

The Devas' messages are always full of optimism and purpose, and express a vibrant love of life. To begin with I was often disappointed by my inability to sustain contact with them, and I felt discouraged when I was too distracted to participate in these exchanges. With time, the feeling of separation began to dissipate and contact with the Devas became sustained for longer periods. I was aware of the Devas even when I was not receiving a message from them. I began to see that this awareness was a vital point of contact from which all communication flowed. One day I expressed my concern to the Devas about the times when I felt unable to contact them. I was sitting in a peaceful spot by a wild stretch of river. The Devas' immediate and soothing answer came:

*Banish sadness! We will refresh and inspire! Come to us not seeking to achieve but to witness and share our worlds. Once you step forth you will feel your tiredness and mental burdens drop away. For in tuning to us you tune to a light which pervades all life. Let life and light in! We do not understand the dense energies which accumulate in human life, for our world is different. There is constant music and song! Listen to the river! Smell the moss and the fragrance! All is shedding forth its light, and when you tune to us, you do the same, for you do so in your way. In the depth of the One-*

*ness of all life, is a deep, loving source, like a pool, endlessly filling and giving. From this we are born, and to this we return. Ebb and flow, but all in light and purpose. We never fade as such, just become directed elsewhere. You have made great efforts to come to us, and this we acknowledge. Wherever you go, you will be able to attune to us again. Enjoy! For the light of life burns in each moment. In your still, less active moments there is also peace, and in stillness and rest you come to us also.*

As my relationship with the Devas has evolved, I have experienced the force of love which has created the beauty and the intricacy of the Golden Web. Everything feels vibrant and charged with life after I receive a message. I begin to perceive the trees, the mosses and wild plants as life-carrying beings, each bearing their unique gifts to life. Not a single flower or stone feels excluded from the process. Slowly my perception of Nature has become more flowing, receptive, continuous and detailed. The Devas have taught me that every living thing has its unique value and expression, and so Nature has become less fragmented as the Devas have increased my awareness of the many evolved forms in Nature and the consciousness within them.

The Devas' messages do not convey a separate reality, but a deeper and more detailed picture of life. The Devas simply wish us to expand our boundaries of perception, and to experience life as it truly is. Nature speaks to everyone in different ways, and the Devas wish each of us to form our own relationship and connection with Nature. The Devas are everywhere, part of everything which surrounds us. We can communicate with them simply by making a conscious connection with the things in Nature that we love. One day I asked the Devas how it was possible to increase sensitivity towards Nature, and they gave the following, detailed reply:

*Your sensitivity was developed to a point when we could reach you at the shared level of con-*

sciousness. We were joined together when the timing was appropriate. In human life, this sensitivity is dependent upon various heightened perceptive abilities. Not all share it, but humankind is more capable of this sensitivity than is usually recognised. We simply infuse all aspects of Nature. We exist in all spheres of the natural world. The spirit of Nature encompasses all aspects of the elements, the earth, the heavens and the detailed energies of the plants, rocks, and forms of life which cloak the earth. Therefore we are not an illusory realm, for we are part of reality, and we exist whether humanity is capable of sensitivity to us or not.

The first way in which people can increase sensitivity to us is to seek us. Stepping into Nature itself is a conscious wish to spend time in our realms. This consciousness reaches us. All reaching forth to us involves an act of will. Whether we respond or not depends on the ability of the individual. But we speak in a multitude of ways. You have also been touched by the profound musicality of this burn, the light of the silver birch leaves turning in the wind, the ancient rock forms which line the pools you have explored since infancy. Your ability to communicate with us grew from this very appreciation of our realms. It became an instinctive response in your life, one which has opened and directed your developments. This IS the way in, and it is built upon. Everyone may follow this path. It is not exclusive.

A sense of oneness with Nature is a true merging with the light of our realms. Messages are not always necessary. We send them through because we need spokespersons to pass on the vital work of mediation and communication. However, as you know, your love of Nature is something you cherish, and value in a deep place within you. For *others this is equally so. We reach forth to all who come to us, and who respect and cherish the greater pattern of life to which all belong.*

*We speak in many ways! Our messages are also carried in sunlight, in droplets of rain, in the magical world of the wildflowers, the depths of the forest and the waterfall pools. We are everywhere and everywhere we shine forth our gifts to life! Recognition of beauty and of the essential nature of life is the true priority. Nature shines and radiates! The gifts and blessings are there for all who have the use of senses and direct them towards us. Love of Nature is the great gift you give to us. It is an exchange. Thus sensitivity to us is not a limited activity, for it is placing an awareness into our realms. We acknowledge and respond. Communication is made in all forms possible — it showers life all around you! This must be communicated. For Nature touches and blesses all, and all are welcome. We leave you with our shower of raindrops and blessings on this, your beloved rock.*

So sensitivity to the consciousness within Nature is something which is innate within us and which we are all capable of developing. It simply involves reaching out to Nature, being conscious of where we are and what surrounds us. The way in is very simple if we choose to use the gifts which are given to us, and is a connection that can be made anywhere, at any time. Although I receive messages when I am particularly still and focused, I am aware of the Devas as I go about my daily life. They continually reach out to make contact with us, to show us how closely our lives are interwoven.

One of the reasons we feel so uplifted in Nature is that the Devas work at a much higher vibrational level than that of human consciousness, one that is very refined, pure and vibrant. When we do carry our worries and concerns into Nature, they often dissipate as we become more attuned to the tranquillity in our surroundings. When I am in a wild place, I often feel a heightened sensitivity and awareness, a particular stillness and alertness to the many different life-forms which surround me. The Devas explain that awareness of detail helps to focus perception and enables consciousness to open and awaken. The Devas explain:

> *In stepping close into the world of detail and beauty, Nature's essence is revealed to you. These steps are part of learning and exploration. Each step changes awareness, within and around you. Awareness of the grain of a leaf, or the the scent of a flower, or the inner pattern at the heart of a flower brings you into our realms and awakens your heart to beauty in the world around you.*

The Devas are at work in all aspects of Nature, in cities as well as in countryside. I am always moved to step into a beautifully tended park or public garden, and to see the way in which people soak up the peace and beauty of the trees and flowers. One summer's day in Edinburgh's Royal Botanic Garden I visited the John Muir Grove of Giant Sequoias which forms a majestic circle in a quiet part of the garden. To my delight, I found someone sitting quietly beneath each tree. One person was meditating, another was absorbed in some writing on a lap top computer, another lay at the centre of the grove gazing up into the great towering canopy of the trees. All that could be heard was the wind and the laughing voices of children in the distance. While the distant hum of traffic was also audible, there was an atmosphere of total, enveloping peace. The Devas came forward with the following message, positively affirming their presence in the city and their joy to be part of a sanctuary:

> *We greet you. What we create here is an oasis and sanctuary within the city where much harmony is created and contributed to those who come here. Have you not noticed the joy and gladness with which people stroll and gambol along the pathways here? All rings with joy! What has*

*been created here is an axis around which Nature can speak its message in partnership with the human world in an urban environment. It is a place to which people are drawn. It may be a wish merely to lie on the grass on a sunny day, but this is good! This too is a point of entry into our worlds. Others come with great sophisticated knowledge of plants and receive inspiration to work closely with their own gardens. Much of mutual benefit and harmony reaches people on many levels. Thus, here in the city, we are glad to be involved in this beautiful sanctuary. You noticed yourself the tranquillity upon entering. We do create our effect here and make our presence felt! It is like bees to the scent of a flower. Why should it not be possible to create heaven on earth, and a sanctuary in a city like this? Love knows no bounds, for it is a law. What is needed is the shift in perception. In coming to us you are part of the pattern and your work will in turn bring others to us. Thus more and more are drawn together for the common purpose of all.*

So by simply stepping into Nature, we are immediately in contact with the Devas. The reality of Devic consciousness is precisely the peace and tranquillity which we experience when we choose to spend those few quiet moments of suspension from activity, or when we walk in a favourite place. The Devas long for us to deepen our appreciation of Nature and to develop our contact with them further. Stepping into Nature, we instantly walk amidst their vitality and light. We may not be able to see them with our physical eyes, but we can experience the harmony and peace of Nature very deeply when we are open and receptive.

The Devas fulfil their work with ceaseless devotion and love. It is love of Nature which brings us to the Devas and mutually enhances our relationship with them. But we are perhaps more aware of the effect Nature has upon us than we are of the effect we have upon Nature. The joy and upliftment we experience in Nature is reflected back to

Nature, to wherever we look or tread, and to wherever our fingers tend to living things. Just as we respond to the Devas, the Devas respond with infinite sensitivity to our thoughts and actions. It is not only important that we spend time in Nature, but that we open our hearts to the creative forces of life. The Devas continually stress the importance of bringing loving awareness to our thoughts and actions. One day I asked them how we could go about bringing change through in ourselves and in our actions. They had much to say about this, and gave the following guidance:

*Firstly, the main step forward is to understand that you are part of Nature, part of us. Mankind has for a long time separated itself from the processes of Nature, having found powerful ways to control and manipulate the environment. This has caused a separation from Nature and a disconnection of spirit. We view this as a dullness, a closing of perception and receptivity which is compensated for by intellectual luminosity and brilliance. But the spiritual realms are not a separate world, they infuse all areas of matter and physical life. As you know, each burn pool is a teeming web of life. Each sprig, each element of life has its own energy, force and power. There is nothing imaginary in this at all! People were much closer to these forces in the past. They were observed and recognised for what they are. It is this relationship which must be restored.*

*The changes can only occur if this notion of separation is removed and banished from the mind. What is missing is a spiritual sense of connection and Oneness, which has lead to a great poverty and diminution of the human condition. It can be restored. If only there could be an awakening to the true essence, spirit and richness of the Nature realms! This involves an embracing of Nature, a commitment to nurturing and also listening to the inner spirit. We speak in so many ways! How can we be heard if mankind does not wish to listen to the inner voice? We cannot get through! But we are here, and you are all part of our realms. We welcome you amongst us, and we give our gift of life to the world which is full of the beauty and forms you so delight to see.*

*So firstly, what is needed is the awakening beyond the illusory barriers of the mind to perceive Nature as the great source of life to which mankind belongs. On a daily level, this simply involves becoming more aware of Nature, recognising its forms. When you no longer feel separated from us, is it not natural to give thanks and to care for what you belong to and love? One action follows from another. When there is unification, when the spirit touches our realms, then there is a harmony, an alignment and understanding. This is a bond and union which cannot be broken once it has formed. It is the damage that has been inflicted by the broken union between mankind and Nature which must now be restored. Once the link is made, action follows. We know that this is an essential shift in perception and not everyone will make it immediately. But it is enough to take a step forward. In showing the way, others follow. It must also be recognised that we call upon you continually. We shape life around you, and we are in your midst everywhere! The forces of Nature are an essential feature of life and matter. All is part of the great energised matrix. Therefore we are continually at work.*

*What may follow is a reconnection of the true relationship and alignment. It is already underway but many more must follow. Much work awaits for the restoration to become complete. When the link is made, it cannot be ignored. You know how you have felt us everywhere, even in the seeming lifeless areas. Therefore the change in perception is lasting. The strengthened bonds become a power, and a new way is forged through. This is the first step.*

*The second step is a movement from within to without, through the unifying power of love. Love is a central, radiating energy, a great force and power. When love is transmitted outwards, in however small or seemingly menial tasks, the work is transformed and becomes a vehicle of service and light. We wish humankind to appreciate and learn this quality of service and action, this way of responding to the work of daily life. What could be more uplifting and fulfilling than to give to the richness of the whole?*

*Each thought, each action that is tended with true love, becomes an entry point into the light realms. We long to be touched by the collective love and care of humanity. If we were able to fuse together, there is no limit to what could be created, transformed and turned to perfection. We do not seek perfection in a limited sense. For us it means fulfilling our potential. Each form we create is built in this way. So we speak not of defined limits, expectations or goals of achievement but a growth TOWARDS, a way of responding. Each mindful and conscious thought is a gift towards this creative process. We try to convey to you, in the simplest of ways, how life CAN and WILL be transformed by the simple upliftment of thought and dedication. The need for this commitment to service is profound, but its effects will radiate far and wide. You know yourself the effects of mutual benefit when we work consciously together. It could not be more simple. We do not seek complicated solutions to solve the great magnitude of problems which afflict the earth, we seek partnership, and partnership begins by the outflow of love, compassion and thoughtfulness to all things, all actions, all thoughts. Directed in this way, there is no limit to what we might achieve.*

*We wish this to be so, for we know what we are jointly capable of creating. We say to you, let love be the motivating factor of life! May it radiate upon you and within you to illuminate all aspects of life and to nurture all that you do and cherish! This we do in our simple, light-filled existence, and call upon mankind to fulfil in its own way, fulfilling the potential of life. These simple guidelines are applicable to all. We send forth our greetings, in honour of all that breathes forth life and of the great Light of creation. Blessings.*

In their communications, the Devas have given great emphasis to the unifying power of love and its power to transform life. One of the very first messages I received from the Devas came from a lone silver birch tree on an empty stretch of moorland. Sheep were gathered under its gnarled and twisted boughs for shelter, and the wind rattled in its branches. I felt a great affection for this tree which I regularly passed on my walks, and I would often stop and sit at the base of its trunk which formed a rounded seat. It was Christmas Eve, and low winter sunlight caught the faded, yellow moorland grasses, warming the surrounding heather with rays of soft, golden light. It was lovely to stand before this beautiful tree and to see so much life illuminated in the wild land stretching into the far horizon. I felt the strong presence of the tree, and a simple message of love came through from the Silver Birch Deva. It was accompanied by a feeling of radiant, loving energy which touched everything around me. The Silver Birch Deva said:

*Love colours our worlds in endless dimensions and unifies all aspects of our activities. Just as sunlight filters through clouds and causes the grasses to turn gold, so everything is interlinked in our world. Nothing is separate. All is part of the Great Creation and formed through love. If you*

*tune into our worlds, with awareness and with
love, you will experience all of the dimensions of
our loving and creative endeavours. For us love is
part of being and is natural. Tune into our worlds
when you are clouded by dark thoughts and you
will feel joy and boundless love!*

Love of Nature is therefore a point of entry into Devic consciousness. The Devas point out that when we focus our
thoughts and actions with love, we participate and co-cre-
ate with them. They refer to light and love as 'the heart of
growth' and stress that the quality of our thoughts has a profound effect on everything around us. It is the conscious
effort that counts, having true reverence for Nature and
bringing greater mindfulness to our thoughts and actions.
The Devas encourage me to increase my awareness of them
whenever and wherever I can, whether walking in the
woods, working in the garden or simply sitting in peaceful
surroundings. One day, I decided to ask the Devas of a
favourite mountain stream how they experienced this love,
how it was directed in their work and towards us. They
replied:

*Love flows out to you as your love reaches us.
We give thanks for the exchange. It is rich and
nourishes life. All life depends on this love, the highest expression of our common divinity, for it is a
giving out from the very centre of life to its very
depths. This is true unity, that which unites all life
and truly binds it together, love which emanates
and resonates from the deepest part. It comes from
the greatest point of divinity within to extend to
nourish all life externally. The richness of your love
knows no bounds. It generates life, for as you step
through our pools, cherishing each tiny flower, leaf
and shade of lichen on the rocks, you make contact with the essence of Nature and your love
emanates out to all that breathes life. From this we
draw our essence. What you breathe out, we*

*breathe in. So when you give us your love, your appreciation and acknowledgement, we receive it as a gift, and we reciprocate by our very being.*

*Love involves being aware of all and embracing all, knowing our interconnection and expressing it. Love enhances life and brings us peace and joy. Your gentle presence here is an attunement with this place for it occupies a special place in your heart. This we know, and this we praise. We are nourished by this exchange and the pattern here scintillates strongly. Let us draw breath together and continue our work of joy and co-operation! Know that the energy of our exchange is embedded within us as it is within you, generating love always.*

One of my greatest pleasures is time spent in the garden. In the mornings I love to walk around the vegetable patch and flower beds, to see how new growth has formed, how the rain has nourished and refreshed the plants overnight, and how the sunshine brings forth the brilliant colours of the foliage and flowers. There are always new developments to observe, as the first peas begin to form, or when a flower opens for the first time. It is always a joy to see a wildflower that has come into the garden by surprise, and I allow them to grow undisturbed wherever they find their place. I take care to acknowledge all this and to give thanks for the Devas' work in bringing beauty to the garden.

The Devas are always eager to assist with practical advice, and they have a lot to say about gardening techniques! Work in the vegetable and flower garden has become an ongoing exercise of co-operation with the Devas. Their input is extremely practical and helpful and makes me aware of what constitutes balanced and healthy plant growth. The Devas have much to say about the inner nature of plant life and as I work in the garden, I feel a more concentrated awareness of the plants as living beings, and a greater involvement with how the plants and flowers are developing.

Working in the garden is a peaceful and contemplative time. I enjoy this quiet time, walking quietly and carefully amongst the beds, noting where the plants need to be tended. I give special attention to the way plants are pruned, or lifted for transplanting, always giving warning when I am about to cut or uproot them. When harvesting vegetables, picking flowers or herbs, I thank the Devas for the healthy growth of the plants, and their presence in the garden. The Devas explain that my presence amongst them is part of the creative flow of the garden and can help the energy to strengthen and build. This makes gardening work exciting, for each time I step in amongst the rows of vegetables, I know I can contribute to their growing vitality through my care and attention. It is a good feeling to be able to give to the garden and to feel part of the growing life in it. It is like stepping into a whirlpool of energy and moving with it, becoming part of it.

The Devas have made me aware that a vital aspect of gardening is not just what is done, but how it is done. At all times, the Devas remind me of the relationship that exists between us, and that the essence of co-operation with Nature lies in honouring this relationship. They continually refer to the importance of awareness and mindfulness in both our perception and treatment of Nature. I listen to the Devas of the garden and ask them questions because in this way I am more connected to life in the garden, and more involved in its care. It is a way of being in the garden, and having reverence for all that grows. The Devas of the vegetable garden described the importance of sensitivity to their creative work in the following message:

> *All is flowing movement and light. When you work with us, at all times tune to this light, and you will be gathered into the creative force of our work. It is important to concentrate at all times with a loving purpose. We are disturbed by unpleasant thoughts and the conflicts which impinge upon the human mind. All creation is a work of love and infinite perfection. If you attune to us, and acknowledge the beauty of life, you will be*

*realising the potential for life and growth on all levels. For while we are concerned with growth, this is the mere outcome of our way, which is one of purification, building of essence and radiation. You can add to this process in the way in which you work. Attune to us at all times in the garden. You will be guided in thought to the right action.*

The Devas are keen to stretch and expand our perception of life to encompass greater potential and wholeness of vision. They say that creativity and wholeness is something that we can achieve with them, in partnership, and that on a wider scale it has the power to bring unity to a divided world. The Devas explain that wholeness is something they seek in their patterns of growth, and that when we aspire to something greater and more whole, the expansion of thought and perception involved immediately opens the possibilities of growth in ways we have not thought possible. The Devas describe the expansion of growth as follows:

*Force is transmitted upwards. Great is the work as life takes hold! The light builds and radiates, and life flows forth. Thus our rhythms and patterns are completed, and life flows. It is like stretching and expanding. Growth is an uptake of energy, transmitted from the forces and infusing the pattern of each living thing. Therefore seek us in our wholeness! Think to what we may achieve! Feel the path of life-force and purpose of each living thing, and you will be united with us in creation. All life is perfected to its own level, and when all is in harmony, great is the song, the rising chorus of energy and life-giving!*

The Devas have encouraged me to banish a limited view of what is possible within a garden and to understand the wider implications of all focused thought and action. The Devas point out that when we attune to a particular species, we are touching not only the essence of the individual plant, but also the species as a collective. So the consequences of our actions are far more widely felt than we may at first realise. What we offer to one plant, or one individual tree, benefits the whole of creation. Since all life is interconnected, the quality of care we offer to the Devas has a very important influence indeed. This view first emerged one day when I was planting out a rowan tree seedling and the Rowan Deva offered the following instruction:

*You must realise that while we have our individual forms, as in the trees you specifically care for here, we are also a collective. Love for ALL trees, love for ALL life, affects our sphere of activity. Thus care for one rowan in the garden is care for ALL the rowan species. Do not be limited to the confines of one tree, one garden, one physical space. By loving and caring for ALL trees, recognising the energy and oneness of life, you may enhance the vibrancy of living life around you, in the garden, by the burn, on the mountain. Wherever you shed your awareness, love nourishes and adds to the whole. If you continue to love the trees and enable them to fulfil their life and purpose, then God's work is enabled. It is the quality with which you fulfil your co-operation that matters. We say, embrace the whole!*

Communicating with the Devas has encouraged me to move from a rather limited view of the world to an understanding of life that is more open and interwoven. The Devas' communications have given me greater insight into the creative process of life, and how consciousness can be opened and expanded to increase sensitivity, perception and creativity, to experience the Divine in Nature, without in any way denying the reality of the phenomenal world. The Devas simply wish us to to experience the world more completely, and to see how everything in the universe is embraced by the radiant light and energy of the Golden Web.

The aspiration and commitment the Devas ask for does not involve separating ourselves from the practical concerns and tasks of our daily lives. The Devas show that a more balanced and integrated way of life is possible and that we can work in new ways, with greater sensitivity, and in closer partnership with Nature. The opening of perception and sensitivity towards Nature is part of developing ecological awareness and putting it into action, through effort and practical endeavour. The Devas highlight the importance of individual thought and action in bringing human activity to a more balanced and sensitive alignment with Nature's energies and ecosystems.

The Devas acknowledge an innate part of human nature which is capable of sensitivity and wise endeavour. They know that true custodianship of the earth and co-operation with Nature on a wider scale is well within our capabilities. They say that each one of us is able to develop consciousness and make a contribution towards protecting Nature and living sustainably. They are deeply encouraging, and readily remind us of the infinite beauty of the web of life which embraces us and sustains us. Our very survival is dependent upon Nature, and it is Nature to which we can turn for courage, upliftment, strength and inspiration to protect the very fabric of life to which we belong.

One day in midsummer, I was deeply moved by the abundance of buttercups in the meadow by our cottage. A roe deer had come out of the oak wood to graze in the meadow, and the sun caught the sheen on its flanks. It looked up and noticed me, then continued grazing peacefully. Walking amongst the buttercups in the bright June sunshine was like walking through a waving sea of golden light. I felt so uplifted to be in this shining meadow of light, and to be surrounded by so many flowers. As I walked through the meadow, with the buttercups brushing my legs, I felt my love flowing out in an open stream, and the great joy of the buttercups to share their life with me. I sat down in the middle of the meadow, and the Buttercup Deva spoke the following message in celebration of life:

*Great is our joy to have you amongst us as we shower forth our positive gifts to life! We have soaked the field with colour, and all is transformed into a meadow of life. Is it not stunning to see the effect of our COMBINED presence here? Does not each add its own very distinct essence to the collective? This we teach you, the sum of the parts, in which life is continually built as a flow and exchange between the many life-forms. Our presence here is a complete pattern, one that has evolved to this unity. In it are contained life-chains, and from us pours forth our richness and vitality, golden with the breath of summer life. It is not just expression of summer, for we are MANIFESTATION of summer energy and light. We are connected to the rhythms and patterns of all that brings forth life. And now in radiant sunshine we open, like millions of hearts, open, flowing, conducting love and light. Do you not uplift to glance upon our field, and walk amongst us? Treasure this golden carpet, let our light and essence flow forth to you, deep in your being, so that we may join together! In perception of us, you experience us.*

*This is mankind's new task, to open and become aware, to fully attune the heart to the gift of divine Light in this world. It is abundant, all around for those who have eyes to see. Thus collectively we bring our gifts to a pitch, flowing outward, flowing forth from the Centre. We are the vitality of summer! Know us as we are, come with our own message and unique essence for the purpose of life! It is time to recognise the interconnection of these things, the pattern of which we are all a part. Therefore we give thanks for our time together. With deep joy we surround the peaceful dwelling with our essence, and wish that you come again. May love abound!*

*chapter 4*

# Restoring the Balance

The Devas have always stressed the importance of our relationship with Nature for our survival and our mutual evolution. They see that our relationship with Nature has become greatly imbalanced and impoverished as a result of mankind's relentless pursuit of material progress. This has caused a growing separation and spiritual disconnection from Nature. We can no longer continue with unsustainable economic growth, with no heed to the future well-being of the natural environment. We must recognise our dependence upon Nature if we are to survive sustainably. The Devas urgently call us to go forward together, in a new and revitalised partnership with Nature, to restore the balance of life on earth.

The Devas point out that the rapid degradation of the natural environment has its root cause in our attitude towards Nature. We have come to believe that we can dominate Nature, to exploit its resources for our material needs and profit without limit. Nature supports and sustains our very existence, yet we are in danger of losing this vital perspective, and ignoring the fact that we belong to Nature, that we are part of a greater whole. This attitude has a long, historical precedence in which human thought and scientific development has changed our vision and understanding of Nature, and our whole relationship with the world around us.

The mechanistic view of Nature, which has prevailed for the last three centuries, was set in train by the Protestant Reformation and by 17th century philosophers like Descartes and Bacon. Descartes was responsible for introducing a model in which the whole universe was reduced to that which could be defined and quantified by mathematical law. Nature was reduced to a mechanism, a machine which could be dissected, studied and scientifically observed according to laws of mathematics and through the use of reason alone. This created a spiritual disconnection from Nature and introduced a new objectivity as science adopted a radically different methodology for observing the phenomenal world.

Francis Bacon further influenced the growing disconnection from Nature by declaring the very aim of science itself to be the control and domination of Nature, thereby subjecting it to human control and mastery. Nature was viewed as a machine that could be manipulated to further humanity's pursuit of knowledge and technological advancement. This mechanistic philosophy developed into a driving force which was to bring revolutionary changes to society and rapid material progress. In the wake of these changes, human domination of Nature became the perceived order of life.

As material progress increasingly dominated human thinking and social development, respect for Nature as a living, sacred organism, with its own laws and powers, was replaced by a view of Nature as a limitless resource to be exploited for the benefit of mankind. This view was compounded by the rapid development of technology and industry. It is this culture of materialism which continues to dominate the political focus of society to the present day.

While material progress has profoundly transformed our world, bringing with it a greatly expanded view of the universe and radical changes in living conditions in many parts of the world, the view that progress depends on limitless economic growth alone is wholly unsustainable in a world of finite resources. The continued exploitation of Nature has led to environmental destruction and depletion of natural resources in order to fuel ever increasing levels of consumption.

We are now facing the consequences of unrestrained economic growth and a thoughtless disregard for Nature. As tribal societies continue to be decimated worldwide, removed from ancestral lands which have been sustainably managed for thousands of years, we lose with them an understanding of Nature which is a key part of our evolutionary inheritance. Nature in the form of a healthy environment is absolutely vital for our survival, yet Nature continues to be exploited and polluted.

Depletion of the ozone layer, global warming, atmospheric pollution, deforestation, erosion of top soil, loss of biodiversity, accelerating extinction of species, pollution of rivers and oceans, declining fish stocks, are all measurable indicators of ways in which Nature, our unique life-support system, is under unprecedented threat. This threat has surged to a crisis point within the span of a single generation, merely the blink of an eye in the evolutionary timescale. The tide must turn: we must transform our attitude, and learn to live sustainably and in greater balance with Nature.

As economic growth and material improvement have become the primary goals of society, the value of the inward path towards spiritual growth and transformation has been increasingly driven to the sidelines, and along with it our understanding of Nature as an organic whole. In such a society, we are easily diverted from embracing our deeper potential as human beings and opening to the spiritual dimensions of existence. Daily life can be consumed by the endless stimuli and distractions of the modern world. Little emphasis is given to spirituality, to the importance of nurturing the spirit as an essential part of well-being, and to encouraging a connection with Nature.

The Devas have described the depletion of inner life and spiritual vision as a 'diminution of the human condition'. As so much time and human effort is directed outwards, towards fulfilling and satisfying needs for material comfort, less importance has been attached to going inwards, to seeking meaning, clarity and direction from the core of our inner being. Less value has been placed on this aspect of human development, or on creating and encouraging a context in which spiritual life is able to flourish. As we have become increasingly aware of the extent of the global crisis, we now realise that there must be a fundamental transformation in vision, focus and direction.

The Devas know that the future balance of life on earth is dependent upon the restoration of a holistic view of Nature in which ecological and spiritual concerns are combined. Our hopes for change should not only be focused on the politics of economic growth, human welfare and global peace, but also on the future of our whole environment. Human progress must be based on a new relationship with Nature, one that involves a greater respect and sensitivity towards the living earth which sustains and nourishes us, the divine web of life of which we are a part.

The Devas indicate that a holistic view of Nature must be restored if we are to bring balance to our own lives and to the world in which we live. The Devas continually refer to the need for us to form a new partnership with Nature, and for us to engage with Nature at a new level of understanding. I decided to ask the Devas how they viewed this new partnership and why it should necessarily take a new form. I wondered if it was to be different from the partnership that humanity has experienced with Nature in the past. I put this question to the Snowdrop Deva, deep within the wood by the cottage, and I received the following reply:

*Partnership is a vital aspect of co-creation. If we are to rebuild and restore the condition of the earth, then we have to re-establish a new sense of reverence and joint responsibility for Nature as a whole. When we speak of Nature, we speak of the inclusive nature of the living and breathing earth. We stand at a time when our focus of perception must go forward, to the future, to that which must be built upon and restored. This involves new principles of co-operation and participation with the Nature realms, from a deeper and more committed place within the human spirit and heart.*

*These principles to which we refer are not different from the long history of partnership that has preceded and predated mankind's present separation from Nature, but are relevant within a new meaning and context. All levels of conscious-*

*ness have evolved, and we stand at a new point of synthesis and understanding of our mutual roles and capabilities. Thus what can now be embraced in partnership takes place in a new and evolved context.*

*We stand at a point of transition in which a new expansion of spiritual vision and understanding takes root in humanity, which includes greater insight into the human condition and that of the planet. Individual suffering and global destruction have been illumined for all to see. What is established now in terms of a more integrated human nature has the capacity to affect a wider sphere of influence. When this insight is embraced, then there is true vision into the greater dimensions of our interconnection and well-being, and new pathways of peace are truly found.*

*Our partnership lies in the new-found sense of a wider self. In global awareness lies the understanding that we form a greater whole. This expansion of awareness is vital for healing, wholeness and renewal. Partnership is merely the bringing together and the cohesion of all living beings in true harmony. Partnership exists at the heart of peace and the creative force of compassion. New partnership depends on the new definition of self in relation to the greater whole; a more expansive and integrated vision based on light, peace, awareness. In such partnership, what one thought, one action creates is created on behalf of the wider community, with awareness of their greater resonance. The actions and thoughts of one individual reflect the principles embedded within that thought and action.*

*What we seek is this wider resonance and expansion; the productive, light-filled nature of life influencing human thought and action in true spiritual unity. In our own simple way, we trans-*

*mit our purity of being forth to the whole. We speak*
*of steadfastness and resolute transformation.*
*Together, in combined strength and partnership,*
*a new cohesion awaits, and a new vision imparted*
*to all. Embrace this awakening, we say! Give to it*
*your all! Place your awareness and commitment*
*towards the highest endeavour and let the new*
*partnership emerge!*

In the present environmental crisis, it is easy for the human
spirit to succumb to a pessimistic view of the future and of
our inability to create change against an overpowering tide
of obstacles. Yet the Devas continually refer to the strength
and creativity of the human spirit. They know that poten-
tially we have the motivation, the inspiration and the ability
to radically transform our relationship with Nature and to
find solutions to the problems which now face us. The Devas
say that vast potential lies within each one of us, if we can
stretch beyond our limited view of life and of our capacity
for change. We CAN bring about change in ourselves and in
the world around us, and we need to become aware of what
we ARE capable of becoming and creating. Restoring our
relationship with Nature is vital spiritual work of our times,
something which touches and affects us all, and which
requires collective commitment and participation.

   The Devas know that human consciousness is capable of this transformation and that through it limitless creative energy awaits to unfold. They have never regarded us
as occupying a separate level of existence, and they long for
us to rediscover the intimacy of our relationship with Nature
and to experience our full potential. The Devas have always
communicated through their messages, the essential unity
of life on earth. They have described how the very essence
of life is peace arising from partnership, and how the whole
of Nature is built upon partnership and interrelatedness. Co-
operation with Nature is therefore a natural form of alliance
in which the Devas long for us to participate. If we place
value on our own well-being and that of other individuals,
we can show the same kind of concern towards Nature. If

we recognise that we are part of Nature rather than separate from it, then it is natural for us to co-operate with Nature.

Nature is central to our existence. If care and a profound respect for Nature becomes the primary motivation, then collectively we will be able to initiate change in the world. The strands of the Golden Web are infinitely reflected and interrelated. We each have our individual zones of influence in life, and unique gifts to contribute to the whole. Lasting changes will not be brought about by political and environmental policies alone, but through individual endeavour and collective aspiration. The Devas have described how powerful conscious thought can be. Each thought, each action contributes to a network of creative endeavour which is capable of changing the whole. The Devas long for us to realise how much we can contribute to the process of change through the context of our individual lives. All personal development and growth of awareness has a wider resonance beyond our immediate selves.

We stand at a pivotal point in our evolution, and ours is the generation upon which responsibility for protecting the natural environment falls. The Devas stress that there is an opportunity to be seized by individuals worldwide, to participate in the process of change. Each step that is taken now is taken for the future. Our co-operation with Nature at the present time is essential for all future life. If we continue to disregard Nature, our lack of reverence for life on earth will become extended to countless future generations. The future of Nature and the entire planet is not just a question of our immediate survival, but also of the continuing evolution of all life on earth.

Once we recognise that our thoughts and actions have consequences which resonate throughout the universe, that as individuals we contribute to the balance of the whole, then we will recognise the responsibility we share towards Nature. The Devas urge us to see that every living part of the universe contributes to the welfare of the whole. The Devas encourage us to view our lives in a wider perspective, to recognise our place of belonging in the Golden Web, and to embrace the implications of being part of an interrelated whole.

Consciousness is continually evolving, and with it our understanding of the universe and the nature of reality evolves also. The development of consciousness means that we are able to develop an increasing awareness of the world in which we live, and to experience greater dimensions of our being. In their message on partnership, the Devas referred to a 'new expansion of spiritual vision' taking place in humanity at this time. We are presently entering a new era of consciousness in which a growing awareness of the interdependent nature of the universe is bringing with it a revived search for the spiritual dimensions of existence. This is occurring precisely at a time when we are becoming aware, more urgently than ever before, of the vital necessity for transformation and a renewal of vision in our world.

The Devas point out that if we are to develop a closer partnership with Nature, there has to be some kind of awakening in ourselves, and aspiration for change. As we work to create balance in our own lives, we bring balance to the external world. As we become clear in ourselves, we can see what we need to do to change our lives, and how to go about it. The more we open and expand within, the more we are able to give to life and radiate outwards. Individual work is therefore a vital aspect of transformation. In their messages, the Devas are calling out to us to become fully conscious and to work for change. The Devas are encouraging us to find constructive ways of developing our awareness and widening our field of exploration, so that once again Nature becomes a powerful and meaningful focus in our lives.

The Devas remind us that when we are moved and inspired by Nature's beauty, our hearts open and we are transformed within. In an instant, our awareness can clear to a state of peaceful receptivity. The Devas also encourage us to look inwards to discover our own spiritual richness and essential divinity. The Devas point out that peace of mind and the presence of the Divine are not just to be found externally, but are within us always, at all times. As we awaken and work to become fully conscious, we become increasingly aware of the presence of the Divine in Nature and in ourselves, so that we merge with it further and further, until we no longer move in a world of duality, with a sense of separateness and limitation. As we come to realise that we are part of the divine web of life, then our growing understanding and insight will flow through us to influence our actions and decisions.

The Devas say we cannot afford to miss the opportunity that is presented to us at this time, and that our relationship with Nature is entering a crucial phase. The expansion of consciousness that is taking place is leading us towards a deeper view of life, and towards understanding the world as it truly is, an interrelated pattern of great beauty and wonder. The Devas' messages beckon us closer to Nature, to show us how powerfully we are connected. The Devas know that when we open our hearts to Nature, we are strengthened, revitalised, and uplifted. They urge us to develop our contact with Nature further and further, so that we can experience the fruits of close partnership, and come to know Nature as a powerful, creative and healing force.

One summer's day, my awareness was led into the dazzling centre and deep, soft folds of colour of the Morning Glory Deva which spoke of our need to embrace Nature and open up to deeper levels within ourselves:

*Gladly we lift to the sunshine and open our beings to the light! We speak of inner light, for life is directed inwards through our centre and out from the centre. We glow and exchange — it is a blending of energies. Growing is not a static process, for we receive this from the forces around us and we give and interact with our own developed fields. It is a meeting and fusing of potential. Mankind needs to recognise the need for diversity of life, for together we aspire to add richness to the whole. We are never arbitrary in that sense, just as you are your own individual self with your own right to life. We cannot understand humanity's desire to destroy so much of life when it is God given and for the well-being of ALL. We are all born of the same source, and the divine Light links us all. Glad we are to bring it to the world with our golden centres and velvet, midnight-blue robes!*

*We endeavour to convey this meaning to you, that life can only be creative when the potential for harmony is recognised at the centre of creative life. Mankind has pushed too much away. It is time to return. Mankind cannot risk losing the opportunities which we present. Our worlds await to teach and give forth. It is a dimension which cannot be suppressed. The mind will not be able to exclude us for much longer. The creative whole to which we belong is full of intelligence, and when you attune to us, you will expand your consciousness by unfolding to new possibilities. We therefore ask you to listen to us and be guided in these important times. All you need to do is ask. Think deep to the centre — let us remind you of the radiance of life and its inner forms! Reach FURTHER! Look DEEPER! All awaits you! Life's richness and beauty will unfold before you! It is our destiny to create together and it is as it should be. Therefore put fear aside and take steps!*

The Devas recognise that we are living through a time of great change, and that we are moving towards a new era of consciousness. The new consciousness is already manifesting in many areas of scientific thought as an explosion of new insights converge on a more holistic approach. These developments in science represent a radical transformation of the mechanistic view which has dominated science for so long. As we stand at an extreme point of balance in the global crisis, the birth of new perspectives opens up a new vision of life and possibilities for the future.

The new thinking is particularly present in physics, where a range of new hypotheses have emerged on the nature of physical reality and of mind in relation to matter.

In the new physics, the relationship between the parts and the whole has been radically re-examined. The universe is viewed as a field of energies, an integrated whole in which the properties of the parts can only be understood in relation to the dynamics of the whole. David Bohm, in his theory of the Implicate Order, has developed the theory that the universe consists of an implicate order which is continually unfolding to form the world as we know it today, and that the whole universe is implicated behind every explicit form. This insight into the interconnected nature of reality has profound significance for our understanding of Nature.

The new thinking implies that we are living in a world that is essentially co-ordinated and integrated. Once more the universe is being viewed as a resonating, interconnected whole. The place of humanity in Nature is also becoming recognised in its true perspective. The nature of mind itself has been seen to play an active part in moulding reality through our cognitive participation. The universe no longer exists outside of ourselves, as some separate process from which we are completely disconnected. In the new thinking, Nature is an evolutionary process of which we are an integral part. James Lovelock's Gaia theory further suggests that the earth is an integrated living system, or biosphere, with its own self-regulating process of life and its own capacity to control the chemical and physical environment. In this holistic approach, the earth is recognised as a living organism, with its own ability to organise and regulate itself.

The implications of the new thinking in science are profoundly significant for our times. The new theories point to the interwoven nature of our world, bringing new perspectives on the meaning, order and purpose of our lives. Our entire vision of Nature turns upon a new paradigm, one that is based on life viewed as an interconnected web of relationships. In this new and enlightened context, Nature and the whole of reality is seen as it really is, as an interdependent unity.

This change of perspective is emerging in all fields of

thought, and is not limited to physics only. Medicine and psychology are also developing a holistic understanding of the human condition and the healing process. Body, mind and spirit are becoming recognised as an integrated whole, not as separate mechanisms with independent functions and separate forms of treatment. Many traditional systems of medicine, such as acupuncture, homeopathy and herbalism are being employed alongside allopathic medicine on a complementary basis, and are becoming available to increasing numbers of people. Alternative treatment methods, which help people to deal with pain, stress, bereavement and trauma, are also becoming widespread. Healing is no longer dominated by one medical system alone, and the diversity of healing arts offers a choice of approaches to health and illness which assist the human condition at many levels.

At the same time, we are witnessing a great expansion in spiritual awareness and orientation. Many people are actively seeking meaningful forms of spiritual practice and personal expression in their daily lives. The wisdom of ancient cultures and mystical traditions is being revitalised and appreciated for the deeper vision of life, and the understanding of Nature on which these traditions are founded. Research into extrasensory perception is showing us that the mind is sensitive to other dimensions of existence beyond those which can be detected by the physical senses. Many people have experienced other states of consciousness, such as 'out of body' or 'near death' experiences. These areas of human experience are now far more openly discussed.

Recognition of these experiences and of Eastern theories of reincarnation are bringing an enlightened and compassionate approach to death and dying. An increased interest in Eastern religions and philosophies points to a bridging of cultures and a beneficial exchange of thoughts, ideas and spiritual practices. For example, Tibetan Buddhism offers a unique approach to attaining higher levels of consciousness, and has introduced many Westerners to the wise, peaceful and compassionate attitude to life that can be gained by training the mind in meditation towards clear awareness.

A re-evaluation of our natural resources is also beginning to take place. It is now recognised that we need to improve the quality of the air we breathe, preserve the purity of our rivers and oceans, and that we cannot afford to contaminate the earth through the continued use of dangerous pesticides and pollutants without harmful results to the health and diversity of all life. Political efforts to achieve consensus on a range of global issues such as global warming, ozone depletion, population growth and loss of biodiversity are a significant development in the environmental movement, especially as political initiatives begin to move the focus of environmental debate from identification of problems towards implementation of solutions.

We are therefore witness to a great groundswell of changing values and perspectives, which, as the Devas point out, is bringing an increase in awareness of the deeper nature of reality, and our dependence upon Nature. The challenge lies in embracing the opportunities that this expansion of consciousness presents. The restoration of balance, for both humanity and for Nature, is something that has to be reached for and worked towards, and involves individual effort and responsibility.

The Devas explain that the opportunity for a new partnership with Nature is particularly pressing at this time because the shift in consciousness is a collective movement which is universally shared. The Devas state that a new partnership with Nature represents an upliftment of consciousness that must be jointly undertaken, and that changes are taking place at all levels of life. Nature is part of the ongoing evolutionary process, continually adapting and regulating itself according to changing conditions. At this time, Nature is also involved in a parallel movement of change, which the Devas describe as a realignment of energies and a change in vibrational rates. I asked the Devas if they could describe the changes taking place in Nature at this time. For the purpose of this attunement, I was seated in a sheltered, undisturbed spot by a moorland stream. The Devas came forward with the following reply:

*We are glad to speak. We speak of a timeliness and an opening. All moves through to a greater alignment with the Light. This we do naturally, for our way of being is rhythmically attuned to the patterns of essence from which we are drawn and with which we build life. We are distinctive and yet we are also shaped by that which surrounds us. All is built within a harmonious framework. When we say new light is absorbed, we speak of a fusion with the Source. It cannot descend unless openings are made. We too have to embrace and expand. This is easy for us, for we are light sources and energy sources. This light is easy to absorb for we are attuned to it, and it is part of our flow and formation, as simply as water falls into these pools. We too open and fill and expand. It is drawn into our essence to be reflected outwards.*

*What does it mean for Nature to absorb new light and where does it come from? All light is born from the One Source. At times light is sent forth to heal and uplift. It is a vibrational change, directed from the Centre to all life. All life receives of this essence. It is part of creation, part of the evolutionary shifts. We enter a new phase of conscious life. All has to uplift. This involves a universal expansion. This means that we too are bathed in this light. We open to it as you open to it also. It is something we are jointly capable of. For us, this opening is a natural response. For mankind, it is a slower process, but the potential for transformation and transcendence into a more unified consciousness involves all. Therefore the potential for co-operation is a reality — a step forward taken by all. This is why we long for mankind to awaken to the glorious potential of the new light, the new energy which awakens all life with the Divine.*

*All is light and creation! The dance of life con-*
*tinues, more brightly and abundantly than ever*
*before. Now is the time when the light shines*
*brightly for all to see and experience. We wish our*
*essential unity to be understood. There is so much*
*perfection and beauty! We are all part of this real-*
*ity and we share the same gift of life. Now is the*
*time to step forward and re-enter the Great One-*
*ness. All moves towards this synthesis, this new*
*point of growth. All is directed towards it. All life is*
*involved in this unifying and upliftment. We are no*
*longer separate and no longer divided. A new future*
*awaits. Awaken! And be glad! For EVERYTHING is*
*infused with the Divine and it blesses all.*

The Devas describe the changes taking place in Nature as
part of a universal expansion of consciousness. The evolutionary process of change constantly leads to new align-
ments of energy within Nature as balance is established. The
Devas imply that changes in vibrational rates are readily
absorbed in their field of consciousness through the continual movement of essence and energy, while for humanity, such changes are integrated more slowly.

The Devas say that the outcome of this opening of
consciousness shall be a greater movement towards unification with the Divine, which has the potential to generate
and promote a more harmonious basis for all life. The Devas
see the present climate of change as a great opportunity for
the re-evaluation of existing values and attitudes, making
way for a more enlightened phase of human development.
I decided to ask the Devas if they could describe the changes
in more detail, and if the changes would be experienced differently by humanity and Nature. I directed this question to
the Devas of a wild, undisturbed part of the garden where
a large, lichen-covered boulder forms a rounded seat, surrounded by tall grasses and wildflowers. The Devas replied:

*We welcome you to the garden. We shall endeavour to answer your questions. The time has come when the energies of the earth receive a new power and light. This is a gradual process, and is already underway. The earth constantly changes and shifts as the forces of Nature adjust and adapt to the conditions and influences which bear upon them in the greater movements. These influence all, from the great to the microscopic. And so when any change comes about, everything is adjusted and finds a new alignment, according to the law of unity and interconnection which weaves the whole of life and the whole of creation together. One movement is shared by all.*

*What takes place is a gradual raising of energy as a new level of evolution takes place. In humankind this is experienced as a new level of consciousness, a development in all areas of thought, perception, insight. So too in the natural world, we respond to changes. A new light and energy pervades Nature, of greater force and magnitude. It is divine light, energy, sent forth to radiate and heal and bless Nature and to assist Nature in the overall movement of change and upliftment. It is a universal process, affecting all of life.*

*We experience these changes as a greater light absorbed into our being. It is a strengthening, a radiating power from which we draw our essence. All our movements are a working of energy and light, and thus the greater light in our spheres of energy means a greater light is shed forth in our pattern, imprints of life and being. Thus Nature itself reflects these fundamental shifts. We adapt ceaselessly to what is around us.*

*The new light is the greater Light of the Divine, which now touches the earth more closely. It is NOW that the pattern on earth is able to receive and absorb this light. Before, the conditions were not suitable. Each movement has its timing and purpose. Now is the time for a greater movement through to the greater Light. Conditions allow this to be so. The imbalance has pervaded too long. Now is the time for the return. Long has this been recognised, and now is the time for the turning of the wheel, the great song of creation becomes renewed in a new cycle of growth. Each plays its part.*

*We must learn to sound a new note together! Mankind has the opportunity to align with the changes and embrace this light, as we do. This is what we mean when we say it is time to form the new partnership. Now is the time for mankind to move through the barriers of perception and to understand the great unity which embraces us all. We may no longer continue as separated units, for all speaks of the Great Belonging.*

*We speak for the unifying of parts. We urge you to understand and join us to begin to view the greater pattern of which we are part, so that true unity and harmony be restored. For this, the greater vision is needed. We speak of our worlds so you may understand. As we reach forth to your consciousness, we meet and unite. Great is our joy and wish for this to be so amongst all mankind, to know the true nature of life and of peace. Blessings.*

The Devas explain that as the shift in consciousness filters through and is integrated by humanity, we will come closer to Nature as we develop a more unified view of the world. The upliftment they speak of is an opening of consciousness towards the true spiritual unity which binds all life, a shift in awareness which will have universal impact. The new partnership with Nature which they refer to represents a harmonious fusion of consciousness between humanity and Nature, and a recognition of our interdependence. I went on to ask the Devas if they could describe how this new partnership would be formed. They answered:

*W*e greet and acknowledge you. These are special times, for the potential for harmony is great, as is the need. Therefore we are overjoyed at our opportunity to share with you. The great movement we refer to is upliftment. It is a step we may take together jointly. Those who become aware will understand and be drawn forward. There is more awareness in your human worlds than there has been and we urge you to come close, and take steps together. It is a question of each playing its part. Just as we send out our tune, so you, as you become aware and give of your essence to the unfolding unity of life, add your own unique vibrant note to the whole. It is not as if we are to be transported by or with you, or you with us in this movement - the nature of life is that all moves TOGETHER. Thus those who are aware of us will move and work more closely with us.

It is a step to be taken, a form of progress. Those who see and know will in their own consciousness understand the potential. The more that we awaken, the easier the transition. Harmony is our natural way, it is the wavelength, if you like, that attunes us to the world, each according to its needs. The greater the communication between us, the smoother the transition. It is worked out on an infinity of levels. All is growing and moving, but the opportunities for steps forward are greater at this time. It is like a magnetism, drawing all forward in unity. We are grateful for the increased levels of awareness we share. It is indeed growing — like a glowing shield, enabling and strengthening the fabric of life. All is blessed and great is the purpose. We cannot emphasise this enough.

We are light-forms — we radiate aspects of light from the Source, patterns of essence and flowing matter which are brought into shape and creative form. All is born from the Centre, so we are *connected by an inner rhythm and purpose, like the centre of a revolving wheel, a point of focus and a place of relativity and connection. What differs now is that greater surges of life pour through. Greater light moves through all life-forms. This affects our imprint as an expansion and adaptation. It is an enhancement of our life. This predisposes us to change — to adaptation and new processes.*

*This also influences humankind in the awakening of consciousness. For light is also awareness, and the consciousness we share is born from our relationship to the divine reality which we share and in which we have our being. This change is registered at a conscious level and filters through, shaping your response as wisdom and understanding is integrated. Thus the mind plays a creative role and is motivated by higher impulses. Soon the consequences of these impulses will be registered in greater wisdom and insight amongst humankind, in the true perception of life and its values.*

*We long for this to be so, for greater insight into the nature of life means greater compassion, unity and peace. We too absorb and reflect these patterns of change and adapt our vibrational patterns to absorb and further our potential at this time. It is a heightening of all that breathes through life. Thus barriers and fixed patterns are shifted as this movement is experienced and anchored. The movement of energy and light is to bring through a greater shared experience, and change must be worked through. Therefore all efforts to work in alignment with the forces of change benefit all.*

*You also ask us how we experience life differently. We experience greater fluidity, greater movement. All is enhanced. We are not static by nature and ours is a continual adaptation to the forces of Nature, the pattern of life to which we belong. Thus it is but a greater enhancement of our pattern and unity, a heightened pulse to which we attune. In this, new patterns are worked. One form of living surrenders to a new, reformed and revitalised imprint, with its corresponding resonances and consequences. All is change and all is light, for the Light moves and blesses all. In this we have much to share and much in common. Soon this will be understood. The new partnership WILL emerge!*

The Devas explain that as our consciousness evolves, the vibrational changes which occur bring with them an increase in perception and an opening of experience. It is this opening of experience which will bring us closer to Nature, lifting us beyond the physical constraints which have hitherto bound our understanding and experience of Nature. This expansion of perception and insight will cause an uplift which will filter throughout humanity as many more come to recognise the unity of life and our dependence upon Nature, and begin to act on their concerns.

The Devas describe a universal upliftment of consciousness which represents a movement closer to the healing and transforming power of the Divine. In Nature, the light of divine consciousness is absorbed directly into the essence of Nature itself. The upliftment which the Devas describe is a simple movement which is integrated and reflected outwards, enhancing the web of life at all levels. It also marks a potential shift in our relationship with Nature, as we move towards ways of bringing our mutually evolving rhythms of life into greater balance and harmony. The Devas' messages remind us how Nature reaches out to us continually, and how intimately interwoven our consciousness with Nature really is.

As I thought of the changes in consciousness which the Devas describe, I wondered how Nature would begin to manifest change at a physical level. I reflected how, for example, a decision to withdraw the use of pesticides on corn crops has swiftly transformed our landscapes into the breathtaking displays of red poppies which have created such a stunning visual impact on our countryside. If simple changes in practice can produce such immediate results as these, I wondered what sort of changes we can expect to see in the future, what the mutual effects and consequences of change will prove to be? I wondered what changes will take place as humanity moves closer to Nature, and if we will feel Nature more strongly as a result? I asked these questions to the Oak Deva from a large bough which curves out over a favourite waterfall pool in a secluded place. From this bough I could see into the very heart of the pool below me where sunlight moved across the water creating dappled, golden shadows and through which trout swiftly darted. The Oak Deva had the following to say on the nature of change and its consequences:

*The nature of change is that it is transmuted at many levels. The development of one level of consciousness necessarily affects the whole. What is felt in one sphere, is experienced in another. The nature of our interrelatedness means that nothing transpires without a wider resonance, and consequences are brought through all levels of life, like a ripple effect, moving outwards, touching and transforming all matter, all conscious life. You see how this takes place continually here, how the character and outward manifestation of matter changes its configuration with the passing cycles of seasonal change, and the workings of the elements. Change is not to be feared. If you maintain a static view of life, change is bound to threaten the boundaries and stability with which your world-view is maintained. We are constantly changing, constantly attuning to the greater rhythms, the energy matrix within which all creation is encompassed. Change passes through us as naturally as clouds pass overhead, bringing rain one moment, hail the next, then clearing to bright skies. Nothing is static or permanent! All is change and flowing movement! While change passes through all levels of our consciousness, we adapt and transmute change by the flow of essence and the shaping of matter. All life attunes to the greater context of life. This is how we come into being. Growth is a materialisation of these transmuted forces — the flow of essence evolved and adapted to many powers and transitional forces. Thus in my being, I bear witness to all change — the flow of life within this burn has shaped all aspects of my being and I continue to bring life through according to the evolved energies which build life here. Therefore when the ground of consciousness shifts, change is necessarily affected at all levels, and material Nature will reflect changes at the core of being. All changes in consciousness are reflected to the wider whole. The evolution of life has formed its nature and rhythms of life from this essential partnership with change. It is not to be feared. It is the natural development of events. Nature will manifest more material changes. As the light-force on earth grows and strengthens, essence becomes more concentrated and refined. Thus life adaptation will become pitched to a new level.*

*This is an ongoing process. It is nothing new! All creation involves a shedding of one form of order for a new integration of life, as the conditions of earth change. As consciousness now changes for humanity as a whole, humanity has a greater opportunity for understanding Nature's rhythms and the interrelatedness of being. Mankind can come to recognise the acute sensitivity to which all life is attuned. When mankind becomes attuned to the finer processes of life and ignorance is diminished, then greater respect for Nature will abound. Thus the nature of change will*

*be recognised, and understanding of living sys-
tems shall be furthered, and a greater appreciation for mankind's role and mediation in the
process of change will be affected. Greater awareness of Nature will affect change on many levels.
This is how greater balance may be achieved. As
we move forward together, humanity will come
forward to respect the forces of life, and the pattern of change can become harmonious.*

*We stand at a vital transition stage. All
changes in consciousness are welcomed. Humanity must LEARN the wider significance of its
impact on earth and the role of individual servi-
tude. Harmonious change has to be worked for.
Together, in partnership, we may strive for a new
future, based on respect and in lasting partnership with the forces of life. Each must work to their
own pattern and plan. Recognition of the value
and influence of individual pattern and purpose
will bring greater opening and alignment with the
Divine. All moves towards the greater peace. It is
to be embraced and respected. Open to understand! Let your lives become masterful conductors
of change! May you play your individual roles in
the furtherance of peace, as each particle of life
and light generates what you so love here. May all
life grow and develop in accord with the Divine!*

In their messages, the Devas communicate the divine aspect
of Nature, the essential divinity within all creation. The Devic
level of consciousness is part of divine consciousness, and
this is why the light of the Divine reaches us through
Nature's purity and tranquillity. The Divine lies at the heart
and essence of all matter, of all reality. It is the living connection with the divine aspect of Nature and of ourselves
that the Devas long for us to awaken to. The new partnership with Nature is a re-awakening to our true spiritual unity.

The Devas continually stress the importance of
human co-operation in the process of change and the active

role we must play in restoring balance to the world. The development of a new partnership with Nature is spiritual work which has to be grounded in practical ways as part of our daily concerns and activities. From a vast rock situated midstream in the powerful flow of a highland river, I asked the Landscape Devas what individuals could achieve at a daily level to fulfil the new partnership with Nature. I received the following reply:

*We wish to convey to you the many levels at which consciousness works, to direct and guide you in YOUR shaping of life. In Nature, light is derived from a central point of focus. All light, all consciousness is directed by a basic relationship to a unifying source and centre. It is this ability to harmonise and unify which shapes all consciousness , all matter and all of existence. Without this focus, we would be without light. Thus all life is moved by an innate urge to establish this essential connection and relationship with the Source.*

*In Nature, this is completed in countless, infinite forms. All reflect the coherence and unity of the Divine. We are all in relationship to the Light. It is our source of life, our basis of being and existence. You too, in the sphere of human consciousness, are drawn forward by the urge of the spirit in your development. You too are drawn towards completion, insight and integration. Your lives are shaped by an ever-expanding consciousness which opens to receive the light of being. We therefore advise you to follow your paths closely at this time. Your relationship with Nature is part of your lives. You have your being and your existence in us. The more consciousness you develop, the greater shall become your sensitivity to the true nature of reality.*

*This is your inspiration, your connection with the Source. The truth and wisdom available to you when you participate with us in your awareness is profound, eternal and clear. We therefore urge you not just to work in partnership with us exclusively, but to embrace your whole life with dedication and commitment towards fulfilling your TRUE nature. Everything flows and becomes possible when higher consciousness is opened and developed. This is not exclusive to the practical concerns of your daily lives. Spiritual work is no longer something to unfold in the corners of life, left unattended and ignored while material reality claims your attention and focus. The lesson to be learnt lies in the present, in clear awareness of your thoughts, your actions, your intentions and aspirations. When light becomes your guiding focus, true wisdom is revealed in simplicity. Your whole life will become a focus of creative endeavour and partnership with the forces of life. When you are peaceful and aware, light will be your source of inspiration.*

*The new partnership with Nature depends upon the peaceful coexistence of all beings on earth. The primary task of humanity at this time is to bring balance to all aspects of human activity. In this, the pure alignment of spirit is an essential element. We cannot stress this more clearly. When you work in light, your work becomes light. In resonance, all is touched. All is dependent upon this essential dynamic. Therefore the first steps must be to develop consciousness, and to grow in the daily arena of your lives. Let everything be touched and benefited by your aspiration and growth, and service to the greater whole! This is the true individual responsibility, the awakening to the sacred purpose of life, to restore and bring all endeavour to completion. In this work, our light, our consciousness works ever closely with you to further the well-being of all. Let light be your guide and focus, and may you be guided at all times by the light of clear awareness! In light may be found the true path of service.*

*chapter 5*

# The Way Forward

The Devas state that a new partnership with Nature must be built upon a greater respect for Nature which will inevitably grow as we come to value and appreciate its profound influence on our lives. The Devas draw me closer and closer to the heart of Nature, to make me aware of the powerful forces of life which are at work in our surroundings, and to feel the presence of the Divine in all living things. Every day, the Devas remind me of the intricate levels of life and consciousness which weave together the fabric of the landscape that surrounds my home; the broad sweep of the fells and the sheltered, wooded burns; the crags and wild stretches of heather moorland; the tiny, magical details of the woodland flora and the mysterious, changing alchemy of the elements.

The Devas draw my attention to their presence so that I may observe qualities of beauty which reflect the essence of the Divine, and increase my awareness of the consciousness within all living things. They reveal the flow of consciousness connecting us to Nature wherever we are, and the constantly shifting rhythms and energies moving life into form. The Devas reach out continually to share with us the miracle of life and the profound beauty of the world in which we live. It is impossible not to feel a sense of awe for the vast web of life, and for Nature's creative power.

I feel particularly attuned to the spirit of Nature and the presence of the Devas in wild landscapes. There is a sense of stillness at the heart of undisturbed wilderness, a feeling of gathered, pure, vibrant energy which resonates freely in the wild, open spaces. My sense of self merges with something vast, encompassing, continuous and alive, witness to the creative force that has shaped the mountains, carved the rocks and the great rivers, and brought forth the trees and communities of wild plants that emerge from the earth beneath my feet. In the stillness and purity of wild places, I am brought to a more peaceful attunement with the flow of life around me and within me.

I experience a great balancing of perspective through time spent in Nature, especially in wilderness areas, where the gentle rhythms of the wind and the rain, the essential energies of trees, plants, rocks and streams surround me with their soothing presence. I have always felt the wild to be a place of sanctuary for the human spirit, where one is able to feel the presence of the Divine in Nature most directly, and where one receives the most profound insight into the mystery of life. Here, the pure energies of Nature remain undisturbed by human activity, and true peace of mind and spiritual clarity may be found.

The Devas say that we must value Nature more, and realise the importance of the life that is contained in wild, undisturbed stretches of land. The preservation of such places is vital for the balance and diversity of life within them, and for their continuing evolution in the future. Our respect for Nature must include a recognition of the value of wilderness for its own sake, irrespective of its usefulness as an economic resource, or as a place of recreation. Our responsibility towards the environment must ensure the preservation of undisturbed ecosystems in which Nature's balance and stability is retained, and from which we draw our deepest inspirations.

The Devas know that it is through our direct experience of Nature that an enduring relationship and respect for Nature is developed. I asked the Devas if they could explain to me the true value of wilderness for humanity and why preservation of wilderness should be an essential priority for the future. I received the following message from the Landscape Devas of a wild mountainside and river which I have frequented since my early childhood. The Landscape Devas replied:

*In light we seek you and reach forth to share our life with you! The true value of wilderness resides in the essential peace and harmony at the heart of life. This is the true spiritual reality of Nature, the pure light of divine consciousness which manifests in the undisturbed and unmediated forms of Nature, working in co-operation to blend, mingle and mould the matter of life. Thus when you step into our realms, you are instantly touched by the reflected peace and depths of tranquillity which shine from the very centre of life to reach you in the depths of your heart.*

*We sing with the purity of life, and our purity of nature radiates light and energy forth! It is this which touches you, and opens you to the light of life. It reaches through, illuminating the core of your being. When you come to us, you step into a pool of illumination, to Nature as it truly is — a flowing whirlpool of life energies, full of swirling, radiant life and eternal spirit.*

*Matter is soaked with this life, the radiant energy of the Divine. You come to know it in the vital force of things you recognise: the flow of water; the buds of honeysuckle draping the pools; the flash of dark green moss below the water, caught in sunlight and revealed to you. Each minuscule particle of matter is soaked in the light of the Divine. It is there for you to see at all times if you are open. It is WITHIN you, your own flower of being awaiting to blossom to the full dimensions of life and potential of being. Therefore when you come to us, you are more open and aware. Awareness of us, of essential beauty, of essential life, filters through and we are experienced by you, just as we experience you, your conscious being, your place of focus.*

*In true wilderness, the exchange of consciousness is magnified. Without disturbance, you know us and come to us more completely. You experience your own nature, uncluttered, and purified by the flow of life around you and within you. Thus in true wilderness lies an essential purity, a power in which the essence of life is stored and radiates outward. You well know how the tranquillity of the undisturbed places reflects the breadth of life and radiates an unconstrained and limitless flow of life. You experience it as a magnitude — as something much greater, evolved and ordered.*

*At the heart of pattern and evolved order, peace is generated. The light of peace is the true reflection of the Divine in all things. All life is attuned to this. The wild land is necessary for the balance of ALL life on earth. Without this unmediated vitality and order, the greater pattern of evolution will falter. The value of wilderness for mankind is therefore more than a sanctuary for the human spirit, a respite from the rigours and stresses of life in a complex, material world — it is its essential nature, its absolute light. Only because of such places can this be experienced in a way that has the capacity to touch the human heart to the light of truth and the greater purpose of being.*

*We wish always to bring you closer to the core of life, the divine essence of life! At the depths of our being, light shines forth from the Centre to infuse and penetrate all life. Stand bathed now in this peace and illumination! Let your spirit and divine nature be revealed until all is united and merges with the Divine! This wild place is our meeting point, our mutual residence within the Great Spirit of Life. Honour it and let the flow of light course though you, opening your heart to the Oneness in which we mutually have our being. In wild Nature, the light of the Divine is eternally manifest, touching all life.*

*May love of Nature and of the wild places be a healing force for all of humanity and all of creation. May the human heart receive the full*

*force of our light and may it be a source of trans-*
*forming wisdom and guidance. May all learn to*
*value the true peace of Nature, the value of the*
*wild places, and work to bring peace to earth.*

In the great rhythms of the earth and the delicate, interwoven patterns of its living systems is a force of pure energy, fulfilling and completing endless cycles and harmonious movements, from the great passages of the sun, earth and moon, to the simple closing of a flower at dusk. We are wrapped in the great web of evolution carrying us forward in the changing flow of Nature's vital forces. Our lives are like drops of water on the surface of a pool when viewed in the greater context of the planet's evolution. Yet our present existence on the earth is an integral part of the overall pattern, for we have evolved alongside the upthrust of the great mountain ranges and the formation of the rivers and oceans. Our presence in Nature is as tangible as the breaking of waves on a shore, the wild call of migrating skeins of geese in autumn, or the flush of green in a spring meadow. Our lives have a contributing impact on the entire evolving order.

In wild places, I find that my sense of time changes as the structuring and analytic activities of the mind drop away. Time eludes immediate definition as I study layers of sediment laid down over millions of years in the rocks under my feet, or the gnarled trunk of an ancient oak tree, or the rhythm of waves slapping against the shore. Time cannot catch the movements of energy that cause bluebell woods to suddenly transform to a mauve sea, or a courgette plant to form a thick, green fruit under its sturdy, umbrella leaves. It is part of the mystery of Nature, how life is laid down before our very eyes in so many invisible and miraculous movements. Everything that is contained within the fleeting glimpses of my awareness recedes to a small dot on the map of Nature's history of evolution.

It was on a wild stretch of Scottish shoreline that my eyes fell upon the tiny, star-like flowers of a small clump of stonecrop growing in a narrow rock crevice. I was intrigued by the plant's relationship to the rock and its tenacity to grow so close to the raw force of the sea and the changing tides. The Stonecrop Deva carried me beyond the boundaries of time which held me witness to its growth by the seashore on that particular stormy afternoon. It spoke:

*Let us take you deeper into the dimensions of reality as you know it, and into the mystery of creation! We draw you in, to the heart of rock, to the ancient patterns of life-forms, condensed and compacted in ageless wonder. We are connected to the beginning and to timelessness, and we therefore take you beyond what you see before you in one instant of the changing world. We grow slowly, but we are moving within wheels of energy and life matter which are as ancient as the birth of this earth, and our going forward is but a continuation of the ongoing work of life on earth.*

*Time fragments your notion of reality and what is valuable. We are adapted in rhythm to this rock, and so our rate of growth is of no significance other than that it is according to its inner LAW. In our essence we incorporate greater sections of relevant force and energy than that which is visible or comprehended by you. The very night sky and winter dark are just as relevant as the light and rain of summer, the warmth of sunshine which bathes us now.*

*We urge you to see through to the evolutionary aspects of Nature, to the processes which have spanned all time to bring us to the world you live in today. We are mirrors of that history and in it is stored the great cosmic dance of creation. This is our strength. Our sense of harmony is embedded in that which has endured and matured — thus we culminate in our being and presence amongst these shoreline rocks. You exist in the here and now, but you also have traces of existence evolved and adapted from the great evolutionary history of time.*

*It is now time for mankind to come near to us again and reclaim responsibility as guardians of Nature, and in true custodianship of the great planet to which we belong. Now at this point of time, the need for communion and unity is vital. It is time to return to the Centre and to become aligned with us to the divine whole. Life is a blessing, a gift, an opportunity to manifest your highest nature and aspiration. This we call upon mankind to recognise, to bring back balance. We give thanks for this communication and we bring our message from the depths of being to reach you in this precious moment of shared time. Each moment is precious! Live fully and experience our universal interconnection! In it is stored the fullness of history and the potential for infinite beauty and wisdom. We wish you well.*

The Devas say that our relationship with Nature is the vital key to the future balance of life on earth. The work of ecological restoration depends upon us fostering a respect for Nature and seeing ourselves as part of a much greater web of life. The impact of humanity's existence on earth today affects the entire balance of creation and the evolution of life for countless generations in the future. The growth of ecological awareness therefore involves an expansion of self and of our shared responsibilities towards the evolving planet. The way forward must involve a return to greater ecological balance and the development of compassion towards all beings with whom we share life on earth.

The Devas have pointed out that such a view represents a shift of awareness towards viewing life in terms of the dynamic relationships between all life-forms and the essential unity of the universe. When we look at life in terms of the relationships between things, we can see how our lives are closely interwoven with the forces of Nature, the wider influence of our thoughts and actions in the world around us, and how we can begin to live more healthily, fruitfully, harmoniously and sustainably.

There can be no doubt that environmental concern is growing as increasing numbers of people are becoming aware of the need to take action to preserve and restore local environments, and to live more sustainably. This growing body of awareness forms a powerful basis of changed attitudes and practices which in turn serves to inspire others to change and become more actively involved in protecting Nature. I asked the Devas how human co-operation with Nature would develop and become more widespread in the future. The following reply came from a bank of deep heather interspersed with naturally regenerating birch and rowan seedlings overlooking a mountain burn. The Heather Deva spoke:

*Listen carefully! Ecological restoration is vital work of our changing times. It is dependent upon a movement and change in focus and priority amongst humankind. Firstly, the work can only be carried out when there is true aspiration towards the welfare of all life on earth. This is a global responsibility. The actions, and creative inspiration of many are involved. Ecological restoration is work which cannot be undertaken until it is recognised that we form a whole. When this is recognised, it will become clear that we all have our part to contribute.*

*In this burn, we work ceaselessly with the changing forces of climate and the elements to give forth life. It is OUR focus, our creative endeavour to do so. Ecological restoration is a principle of life. Human engagement is an essential component. This is why we seek your partnership. We cannot work constantly to adjust to the forces of life and integrate them if mankind pursues the present course of destruction and imbalance. It is bringing everything out of line, and affects the profound order of life. Thus we encourage you to work individually in your own spheres.*

*We wish to communicate to you our hopes for the future. In times to come, humanity shall awaken in spirit to the pure essence of Nature. Each will find their OWN connection. Each has their own connection with Nature, an inner linking which carries them to a point of contact. It does not matter HOW this takes place, for the paths to inner awakening are many. What matters is the individual effort, the reaching towards and the aspiration. We witness already a collective movement towards a more inclusive spirit amongst humankind. Progress may seem slow, but progress can only be made when all seek the connection. By this we mean there is a need to understand the forces of change and to seek meaning in the developments which are occurring.*

*At the heart of change, opportunity awaits to be embraced. We offer this to you continually. Nature calls and touches upon humanity in all ways possible. Your response to change is slow but it has begun. It does not matter that small steps are made initially. It is more important that the foundations of awareness are laid. The more who come to recognise the nature of our interdependence, the greater the flow of change and upliftment shall become. All moves towards a new point of synthesis. It must be integrated, brought to light. The awakening must be strong, a radiant focus and inspiration. When this is so, many more will recognise that new paths forward exist, and that humanity has for too long closed its doors to its true potential. Harmony with Nature is a harmony and an embracing of spirit, of all that breathes, lives and exists. The divine Light embraces all. When you recognise that we are all One, then nothing can break our fundamental bond.*

*The coming to us is of utmost value and significance. When you see the profound reality of*

*Nature, your vision and insights will expand to embrace a great appreciation of the divine workings of creation. The co-operation will only become more widespread as people are moved in their hearts to respond, to nurture and care for that which they are part of. Therefore the awakening of heart and spirit is central to the upliftment of ALL life to a new relationship and synthesis. We wish all to come to know the radiant light and beauty of our realms! The pure spirit of Nature touches all, and all are welcome. Listen! And hear our messages reaching out to you in clear waters, the grain of rock, the delicate buds of spring. All resounds with life and purpose! May we unite and celebrate the true light of the Divine, which embraces all.*

The Devas stress that our partnership with Nature is innate because of the shared basis of all life and because together we form a whole. The Devas point out that when we realise our interdependence, then we can begin to work towards restoring wholeness and balance to the world around us. It is this thinking that must be at the core of the new partnership with Nature and forms the way forward for the future.

Sometimes it seems difficult to find the inspiration for wholeness in the turbulent world in which we live, for it is not reflected in the reports of warfare, social conflict and environmental destruction which reach us through the media and usual information channels, and it is not easily found in the crowded, traffic congested city streets. But the desire for change exists in the hearts of many people who are becoming deeply concerned about the fate of the earth, who deeply value Nature and recognise that WE must change, to contribute to the process of restoration and a return to balance.

At a grass roots level, increasing numbers of individuals are becoming involved in taking action to protect species, local habitats and to campaign for greater emphasis on environmental issues. It is this focus of attention, this groundswell of public concern and feeling which represents a turning point in human values, and a growing aspiration for a more holistic world-view and treatment of Nature.

The Devas see human involvement in the process of change arising naturally as more and more are drawn forward to act upon their inspirations. The fact that so many people feel so strongly about environmental issues is a real sign of a growing recognition of the urgent need to protect our natural environment and conserve our wild places. The Devas remind us that the process of change can only evolve through our individual efforts and through fulfilling our individual responsibilities. The Devas say we must not lose sight of our creative capacities and the value of individual endeavour.

On a recent visit to Spain, I visited an industrial city on the north coast, where steel works belch clouds of chemical laden gases into the atmosphere, forming a thick haze of pollution over the valley. The stench in the air was so great that my eyes watered and I could taste the chemicals in my mouth. The smog hung over the town, and spread far into the adjacent valleys and countryside. At night the lights and noise of the steel works flashed and thronged like a vast, monstrous machine, while cattle foraged peacefully in the meadows of small farms on the immediate outskirts of the city.

I was very struck by the proximity of these farms and meadows to such heavy industry. I wondered whether the grazing was affected by the severity of the air pollution, but I was surprised to see many wildflowers growing in this area. The Devas of the meadow where I stood overlooking the steel works spoke of their great resilience, reminding me to acknowledge what lay before my eyes and not to disregard the power of Nature to persist in inhospitable conditions. They came forward with the following message:

*We grow because we are given life. Life-force is active within us and directs our growth. It is this activity which brings out of seemingly hopeless situations the promise of something whole and formed. It is easy to see the extent of destruction created by man's interference with the balance of Nature. Much that meets the eye here speaks of desolation and desecration of the pure. But we wish to remind you that in OUR sphere, life continues to the extent that it cannot be entirely extinguished. How else could we grow? It is not entirely without hope or promise, however great the need for restoration and balance. Is it not worthy of reflection how we have managed to come to fruition amidst the overwhelming force of pollution and denial of life? For in us lie the seeds of miracles, the essence of life diminished, yet perfect in its forms. Never disregard that which is present! Look always to see what lies to be built upon, to be recovered and given back to the whole. The parts are as essential as the totality, and nothing is to be excluded. Thus in industrial landscape, Nature is also present and has its voice. We wish this to be remembered and brought to your attention. This enables an inclusive and broader vision of life than first meets the eye, and insight is lead beyond the immediate boundaries of perception.*

I was glad to be reminded of Nature's fortitude and power, and to feel the essence and vitality of the wildflowers pouring into the meadow despite the proximity of industrial pollution. Even so, there are limits to Nature's ability to flourish, or even to survive, in extreme conditions. Sadly, there are countless examples of how the environment has been degraded by human activity, with natural habitats being destroyed and species driven to extinction. In the Czech Republic, I have seen huge areas of forest devastated by acid rain in the Northern Bohemia region. This area of central Europe has some of the most concentrated atmospheric pollution to be found anywhere in the world, and the catastrophic impact is profoundly shocking. Where there were once villages, farms, and woodland, there are now one thousand square kilometres of open cast mine, which has utterly removed any trace of Nature.

The Spanish wildflowers clearly demonstrated to me the importance of preserving the ecological integrity of the environment so that the natural balance to be found in traditionally cultivated land is not wiped out by unregulated industrial activity. There has to be a sensitive balance between protecting Nature and producing the goods and the food which we need in order to live. Achieving the right balance is one of the greatest challenges facing us today. The difficulties sometimes seem to be insurmountable, but a way forward must be found in order to restore the balance on which all life ultimately depends.

The problem of finding a way of living sustainably is present in almost every aspect of human activity, and none more so than in food production. Pollution of food and drinking water due to widespread use of chemicals is causing increasing public concern. Artificial fertilisers, pesticides and herbicides are used to improve the appearance and size of produce and to increase crop yields, but the chemical substances used in them are retained in the food and the land in which the produce is grown. Since the Devas represent the pure, essential energy of Nature in its different forms, I wanted to ask the Devas how they are affected by the use of pesticides, how they view their usage and their long term effects on the environment. I asked this question to the Strawberry Deva, and I received the following response:

*The movement of life is a creative, powerful process in which many contributing forces are balanced and aligned. The manifold of life is a bright cloak, a formation of essential energies drawn together for the purposes of creation. All growth is an alignment with the essential processes of life, and the influence of those forces which pervade in a given environment. All life is a process of adaptation to that which surrounds. From this the essential harmony of Nature, our balance, our growth and health of being is derived. We slot into the creative pattern of life. We do not seek to dominate at the exclusion of other life-*

*forms, to push our creativity forth at the expense of other communities of life.*

*Mankind pushes our creativity beyond the limits of what is healthy and natural to us. By coating us with chemicals as a form of control, everything is thrown out of balance and alignment. Life is forced to ensure the exclusion of other species, and this is a violation of the natural balance, the threads of life which form ecosystems. It is stripping away Nature's own defence mechanisms in which the balance of life thrives, and is mutually controlled and adjusted. Life-force is weakened at the expense of productivity. Do you not see that productivity lies in the essential quality and vibrancy of essence, in nourishment and energy that is naturally drawn from the soil, the rain, the air, and the sunshine?*

*We wish mankind to recognise that the diversity and balance of life is seriously threatened by practices which over-manage and control our growth. We do not need pesticides to complete our growth and maximise our potential for life. If only mankind could see that co-operation with us can be equally productive without such substances! The essence of living things contains a vital energy which in unmediated purity is life-enhancing and nourishing. Pesticides and chemicals deplete our essential vitality and purity. Balance is not created by promoting form and productivity above the essential quality of vitality.*

*The residues of these chemicals are lasting. They penetrate and accumulate in fine particles, altering the formations of strands of life which are essential for our vitality and patterning. Damage is not confined to our sphere alone, but has consequences in the wider rhythms of life. Your own vitality and energy is depleted and altered by the accumulation of these substances within you, and the balance of your well-being is also affected.*

*Nothing exceeds balance without due consequence. We communicate to you our desire for more harmonious and sensitive methods of production which respect the combined forces of life that contribute to the health and balance of the whole. Our wish is to grow in accord with the patterns of life that have evolved through refined adaptation, not with patterns of growth that are imposed upon us for the purposes of excess growth and production. The balance of life is far more finely attuned than is recognised by you. We wish to be cultivated without interference to our essence and substance of being. Abundance is our nature - life is not improved by external forms of control! We urge a return to the whole, the refined and the pure, the flow of life that brings us to our natural coherence and manifestation. This is our essential nature , and this is how we wish to continue.*

Sophistication of technology has brought many changes to agriculture. Intensive monoculture crops now widely replace the varied vegetation of traditional mixed farming and the biotechnology industry now uses many advanced techniques for developing agricultural crops. In genetic engineering, plant genes are identified and extracted from cells in order to produce plants that are resistant to certain fungi, viruses and pests. Advanced techniques are also used in horticulture for micro-propagation, where explants, or plant tissue that has been extracted from a plant, are divided and grown on in test tube conditions. This method is used to create new cultivars, to increase the stock of rare plants, to produce plants that are otherwise difficult to propagate in quantity, and to produce stock that is disease-free.

The Devas have made me increasingly aware of Nature's sensitivity to human interference and I asked them how they viewed this use of technology and the effect of such practices on their creative activities. The Tomato Deva replied:

*F*irstly, you must begin to see that within Nature, a wider pattern and coherence operates to carry evolution forward. To this end, each constituent part has a unique position within the network of life and operates within its own defined field of consciousness. The diversity of life is what contributes to the adjusting overall order, the balance of ecosystems and their perpetuation. This balance contains a power; it is highly ordered and its response to maltreatment is sensitively tuned.

Genetic engineering may represent one form of mankind's growing capacity to dominate and manipulate Nature for particular means, but it does not represent a balanced approach towards furthering the health and protecting the diversity of the wider environment. It may be considered a feat of innovation and creativity of a scientific kind, but humanity must learn to see that distortion and control of Nature only serve to weaken the balance of the truly evolving order. While on the one hand, disease-resistant plants lead to a particular strain of dominant growth, it is at the expense of naturally evolved strains which have developed a harmonious pattern of life in accord with other species. Why seek to further one thing, while neglecting the rest?

The growth of human knowledge at times surpasses Nature's ability to integrate the changes that are imposed upon the earth through the sophistication of such techniques. It is a form of reduced vision, to concentrate upon such refined mastery of technology while the balance and integrity of the wider environment is disregarded. Our essence is drawn towards a particular formation, and we bring towards us a harmonious and co-ordinated field of energies to promote healthy growth. Nothing can ever be created in absolute isolation from the natural forces of life *and without regard for the harmonious basis upon which all life is ordered.*

*We secondly question your motives for employing such techniques. Sophistication of technology to protect endangered species, or to create beauty is harmonious with Nature as long as the intention and purpose of such activities is the furtherance of life, and the contributing balance of the biosphere. What is often lacking in such activities and in the developed scientific environment is respect for Nature, a regard for the broader context in which such industry must be firmly placed if Nature's balance is to be protected. True co-operation with Nature is based upon respect for the environment as a whole, and care for each of its constituent parts. In some cases, your use of advanced techniques is employed with great sensitivity and care towards the protection of particular species. But where one species is advanced at the expense of many others, the cohesion of Nature is often threatened and damaged.*

*Now is the time to take seriously our calls for a reappraisal of human activity in Nature, to cease exploitation, desecration and control of Nature, and to view living systems with regard for their integrity and essential value. Humanity's view of life must expand to see the wider consequences of such activities, and to consider where they lead Nature in the future. The future must be based upon your applied wisdom and caution, to the direction of your endeavour towards furthering that which benefits creation as a whole.*

The Devas always encourage us to think in terms of wider patterns of influences, and to see the consequences of our activities in a broader context. In their view, ecological restoration is dependent upon a fundamental respect for the integrity of living systems and the balance of life within them. Global biodiversity and ecological balance is the outcome of local biodiversity and ecological balance. Everything is connected and we all have responsibility for protecting Nature and the diversity of life with which we share the earth.

Ecological restoration is not something that has to take place somewhere else as a problem for others to tackle; we are all part of Nature, part of the ecology of the planet, and we share the same living system. The Devas say it is time we began to realise the harmful impact of mankind's often indiscriminate exploitation of Nature and begin to adjust our activities accordingly. Each of us contributes to the balance of the whole. The Devas call upon us to see how our thoughts and actions have a ripple effect on the waters of collective consciousness and why the growth of individual ecological awareness is so important for the balance of life in the future.

The Devas are eager to assist with all efforts to co-operate with Nature and to protect the natural environment, and they welcome our partnership with them. In practical situations, the Devas often present their view of life, which places immediate circumstances in a greater perspective. Their consciousness is always pure, positive and life-enhancing, and they always encourage a constructive approach to the tasks we undertake.

One autumn, I was working as a volunteer with a conservation group in an old oak wood. We had been working to clear the brash of a commercial plantation of pines that had been interplanted amongst the oaks. At the end of the day, our group felt quite despondent about the lack of progress we had made, the amount of time it would take for these particular oak woods, let alone the many other dying oak woods in the area, to be brought back to life. The Oak Deva came forward to communicate the following message of encouragement:

*In reconciliation we seek you. The management of these old woods requires action of a two-fold nature. Firstly, you must begin by perceiving the restoration of the whole, the potential for complete unity which lies within this area to unfold into life. Without this perspective, the purpose of all action is lost. Without the view of the growth of this wood from what it has evolved to be in the present to be taken forward to a complete unity, you cannot begin to see the interrelation of the parts. In action this means beginning to see the purpose of individual tasks, individual thoughts. Your efforts here to sustain and restore these woods may at first sight seem limited in effect. But it has no less been time spent amidst an evolving, living wood. ALWAYS we are in partnership with you, whatever your task, whatever time factor is placed upon your contact with us. All is not so seemingly fruitless! We gladden to see your resolve and determination. This itself creates progress. This you communicate also on our behalf. Care and dedication are of utmost value if we are to begin to restore what we have the potential of creating.*

*Secondly, you must begin to perceive the much greater pattern created by your influence in these tasks of co-operation. You show the way and create a way for others to follow. Thus what you determine has an influence on those who will follow. The way is cleared in establishing the work of restoration and enabling others to come and continue work of true value and creativity. All is not lost.*

*We say, always attune to the greater purpose, however far-sighted, however limited it seems at first sight. For we are active everywhere, and everywhere we have the potential to bring harmony and unity to areas of life and vitality. This is our view. We give thanks for your care, commitment and effort. Be at One with us.*

I am often helped by the Devas' positive attitude to life. They help to transform seemingly hopeless situations which generate a feeling of despondency with an insight that leads to a wider and more compassionate view of the situation, in which other possibilities and courses of action exist. Always they encourage us to stretch our view of life, to work with vision towards creating a balanced and harmonious environment. I often ask the Devas how particular tasks in the garden should be carried out, and how we can generally lessen our harmful impact on Nature. For example, the work of conservation groups I have joined has sometimes involved cutting back the young or invasive growth of non-native species in order to restore woodland to its natural state. Clearing, lopping, and felling is sometimes a necessary part of the work involved in restoring ecological balance.

The Devas stress that HOW we undertake this work is of utmost importance, so that damage to individual plants and trees is minimised. The Devas say that plants are able to recover more swiftly from the effects of cutting, pruning, or lifting when we pay careful attention to our thoughts and intentions as we work. Working in conscious co-operation with Nature involves encouraging a harmonious flow of energy between ourselves and the living things which we are handling. When plants are cut or pruned, it should be done bearing in mind the purpose of such action, and always in awareness that we are handling living forms with their own life-force and energetic sensitivity.

The Devas continually emphasise the difference that is made when we pay careful attention to the way in which we do things. This was brought home to me by the Aspen Deva. We had cut root sections from a small stand of aspens in order to propagate them and increase the number of aspen stands in an area of forest. The Aspen Deva encouraged me to see that the cutting of root sections could be done in such a way that recognised the Devas' pattern of growth and honoured its reproductive capacities. The Deva reminded me that while aspens had been depleted in the forest, they nonetheless contributed to its overall diversity, and that we should bear in mind that their numbers could be significantly increased in the future. It was therefore important to take the root sections bearing in mind the purpose of restoring wholeness to the forest. The Aspen Deva spoke:

*A*ll *is at peace. All radiates in unison. Your thoughts and wishes reach forth to us in our isolated splendour, as we draw you to us. We give thanks for the exchange. Although we appear isolated, yet we form our own unity here, at one with life around. Our roots extend our pattern outwards, extending and furthering life, and, with its own distinctive identity, it creates a space and energy of its own in this wood. Thus, in trembling, golden richness we add our note to the wood, to the distinguished and mature patterns of life which have evolved here. Each section adds its part. One is not without the other. Each fragment is not just a remnant, but a contribution to the whole.*

*We say to you, think not in terms of what is lost, depleted and emptied, but of the song of returning life — the presence of the many parts, which may yet blend and extend forward as we do, secretly furthering our pattern, fulfilling our destined purpose within this small burn. Thus Nature continues in its patterns and rhythms. Your awareness and understanding of the diversity here is indeed a blessing. You join in our rhythm and purpose. Joined and connected to one, you perceive the whole. And thus all is united. This is the true purpose — co-operation and unity with the whole. And so, all sings of this Oneness and harmony is restored.*

*Think to the larger pattern always and nurture your own individuality, as we cherish ours, and pour forth our own unique essence for the purpose of life! We give our essence to you gladly; for the gift of life, when truly acknowledged and understood, is a true gift. We give thanks, and shower our blessings upon you, in praise of all.*

I always find inspiration from working in the garden, learning how the plants grow and watching their lives unfold as life in the garden evolves and matures. I love the feeling of contact with the living world of the garden: feeling the warmth and moisture of the soil around the plants as I work; hearing the throbbing of the bees as they bury deep in the blossoms of nearby flowers; sensing the soft brush of air and whirring of small birds' wings as they fly about the garden on their business.

The garden throngs with activity as the warmth and maturing energy of summer draws the life of the garden to a fullness. I feel close to this vital energy as I work in the garden, and my perception of Nature is focused by my involvement with the growing plants and flowers. Time spent amidst the flowers and vegetables is deeply soothing and uplifting; tending to the plants makes me aware of the presence in the garden of living forms with their own responses to the changing weather and seasons.

In a similar way, I have greatly enjoyed working as a volunteer with conservation groups. My understanding of particular species and ecosystems has been broadened by the experience of working in different environments and participating in the various tasks which are involved in restoring and protecting them. I have particularly enjoyed working as a volunteer for Trees for Life, a Scottish charity which is working to restore the native Caledonian forest of the Scottish Highlands.

Native pine woods originally formed extensive forest cover throughout the Scottish Highlands, and today only 1% of the original pine woods still survives. The climax species of this once great forest is the Scots pine, but there are other species present such as birch, rowan, aspen, juniper and oak. The remaining areas of mature forest contain a rich mosaic of ferns, mosses, lichens and berries, providing food and shelter for many bird, mammal and insect species. The profusion of life found in the surviving areas of forest contrasts sharply with the bare mountains and glens where the trees once flourished.

The Caledonian forest has been severely depleted through deforestation and the consequences of human impact on the land. Since neolithic times, the land was gradually cleared for agriculture and timber for the growing human population. Damage to the original forests accelerated to a critical point during the last 150 years due to intensive overgrazing by sheep and red deer, whose last natural predator, the wolf, became extinct in Britain during the 18th century. Grazing pressure prevents remnant pine woods from naturally regenerating. The Caledonian forest is so seriously degraded that there is a risk of it dying out altogether in the next few decades if no action is taken. This irreversible loss of a unique habitat now seems to have been averted by new policies and the combined efforts of conservation organisations which seek to preserve and restore the Caledonian forest to its former glory.

Trees for Life is an organisation which works with government agencies, private landowners and other conservation groups to regenerate the Caledonian forest and to restore deforested land. As well as serving as a model for forestry projects in other countries, Trees for Life helps promote the protection of forests and the work of conservation groups worldwide in an informative calendar and diary which are produced each year.

The ecological restoration work in Scotland is focused in three main areas, and much of it is carried out by volunteers. Firstly, fenced enclosures are created to keep red deer out of areas at the edges of existing remnants of forest, so that seedlings can naturally regenerate with protection from grazing. Secondly, native trees are planted in deforested areas to extend the area of forest and to ensure seed sources for future regeneration. Thirdly, areas of original forest that have been planted with non-native species such as lodgepole pine and sitka spruce as a commercial crop, and which destroy the natural character and balance of the forest, are cleared of non-native trees in order to allow natural regeneration.

Work weeks with Trees for Life draw people of all ages and backgrounds and from all corners of the world to participate in the practical work of restoring the forest. Some volunteers have never set foot in the Scottish Highlands before, and some have never experienced living in a remote location in basic accommodation without electricity or running water. Some volunteers come with considerable experience in conservation, forestry and ecology; others come to draw inspiration and refreshment from a new learning experience. What unites everyone is an eagerness to work with the trees to ensure the survival of the forest, and the willingness to contribute, time and energy towards the preservation of a unique and precious environment.

The weeks are both an educational and an inspirational experience; an opportunity to learn more about the forest ecology, and to experience at first hand the joy of working in direct co-operation with Nature. I am moved to witness the concern that is shown by volunteers towards the future of the forest and other wild corners of the earth; to see the tremendous results of regeneration in areas which have been recently fenced off; and to share with volunteers the inspiration of this work. One emerges from the forest with a profound awareness of the value of the trees and the work that is being carried out, and the importance of preventing further damage to natural habitats and the diversity of life within them.

The Scots Pine Deva spoke to me one day of the broader significance of the work that is being carried out in the Caledonian forest. It came from a magnificent old tree, situated on a high ridge from which I could view the majestic sweep of forest over the surrounding hillsides. The Scots Pine Deva said:

> *I speak of great strength and magnitude. What lies before you is an evolved and vibrant pattern of energy, worked through to become the myriad forms and shapes which characterise the Great Wood. It is of utmost significance to the broader nature of the land. In restored fullness, this mountain area forms a vast and distilled diversity, harbouring many forms of life. The animal kingdom*

*shelters and takes its life from this wood.*

*We are at the point of transition. Now the vision extends to allow the pattern to be carried forward. This is a step forward on behalf of Nature, humanity and the greater whole. The awareness of the value of our essence and glades is a step forward into the realms of true co-operation with the Nature forces and with Pan. Man's role is this balance and co-operation with the kingdoms of Nature. The recognition of these patterns is of utmost value. Now we stand at a time of recollection, for the force and energy of these woods to be perpetuated in seed and in vitality and essence. Your cone-gathering is part of the process, part of the great chain of life which radiates outwards.*

*In the depths of our ancient and evolved life, we pour forth our wisdom and strength. Rest upon it. Know that in this wood is gathered a multitude of vibrant beings. All come forward to bless and work with you. The Elementals and the Nature Spirits are aware of your endeavour and aspiration — they welcome you. Jointly the richness of life is multiplied. Thus seed and essence scatters and creates form, and the fabric builds — matter upon matter, energy form within energy form. All is united in the great Light which shines in and through all living forms. And thus in praise of magnitude and essence we stand and anchor this force in the breathing rhythm of the wood. Know that each seed contains this pattern, imprint and potentiality. Nothing is diminished. All awaits and joins in the song of life-building and the great work of creation!*

The restoration of the Caledonian forest is a key conservation programme in the United Kingdom. The work of Trees for Life and other organisations represents a positive step forward to ensure the survival of our native forests, with enormous benefits to ecology and wildlife. In view of the threat to forests worldwide, this work is an enlightened example of the practical work that needs to be carried out nationally and globally. Seeing the results of a day's planting, and areas where natural regeneration is visibly underway, is a greatly heartening experience. The process of regeneration will take many years, but there is the knowledge that the vital work of restoration has begun before it is too late. At the end of a day's work planting, the Scots Pine Deva emphasised the importance of human involvement in the work of restoration:

*In essence, I greet you. My return to these bare slopes marks a new breath of life, which shall resonate far and wide. It is timely, for long we have been disregarded, and through the process of IMBALANCE with Nature, man's ignorance and lack of co-operation with us, has led to the bareness and barren slopes which sweep before you, devoid of tree, devoid of the potential for life which once grew in abundance here. All longs and awaits for this glorious revitalisation, to fulfil our true purpose in unity.*

*This we do continually, for we continue to regenerate and shed forth seed, as is our natural rhythm and purpose. But it has not been balanced by man's USE of land here. We reach forth to you in gladness for the task undertaken and the endeavours carried out with dedication and true love. When you work in this way, you perceive the true wonder of Nature, our vitality and resilience — the strength and vigour of all life, stored in essence within the land. And so, by stepping into this dance of life and creation, you add your own note to the growing song of life. With your care and co-operation, joy pours forth in abundance — life shines and radiates in all corners!*

*We gather together in this joint task. As your love and service of Nature leaves us in tune with the land in which we belong and take our place, so you, in your own ways, carry this joy which shines and glows, highlighting the light within each one of you. Thus we exchange gifts. We give thanks and express our joy to go forward together.*

Trees for Life is an inspiring example of how human beings can become effectively involved in the work of ecological restoration, through working in close co-operation with Nature to heal areas that have suffered as a result of human impact. Organisations like Trees for Life rely upon volunteers to help achieve their aims, and show how much can be achieved when groups of people are drawn together to act on their concerns and help protect unique environments.

The Devas recognise the creative energy that is generated when people reach out to Nature, whether this be to practically benefit the environment in some way, or for personal, spiritual enrichment. It is growth of awareness and appreciation of Nature that leads us to become more involved in learning about our natural environment, helping to protect habitats and ecosystems, and adapting to more sustainable lifestyles. Nature touches and inspires us in many ways, calling us to come closer and to deepen our relationship with Nature. Developing interests which take us out into Nature more, such as walking, organic gardening, building a garden pond, learning about wildflowers or bird life: these are all ways in which we experience greater intimacy with the natural world, and through which our interest in Nature is stimulated.

As we become more conscious of Nature, we become more aware of the contribution we can make to protecting the natural environment. There are many ways in which we can become practically involved in the work of ecological restoration, both locally and at home. Each of us will be drawn to concentrate our efforts in different ways. All positive action has greater significance when viewed in relationship to the collective process of change. As we work to live more sustainably and harmoniously with Nature, we help create balance in a much wider context. Through recognising our interdependence with Nature we can begin to see human actions and individual endeavour within a much greater perspective. The Devas constantly encourage us to view our activities for their true creativity and value, and to seek practical ways of acting on our deepest concerns.

Love of Nature opens our hearts to beauty and brings us greater peace and harmony in our lives. Nature is the great healer; all traditional systems of medicine reflect different aspects of Nature's healing laws. Our task now lies in co-operating with Nature to assist the healing of the wounds we have inflicted on the earth, to bring our lives into harmony with Nature in a new, constructive partnership. The Devas' promise of co-operation with Nature indicates that the future will be built upon the fabric of our individual lives, through the creative energy of our endeavours, and through our aspiration for a new synthesis of values and a healthy natural environment.

The Devas remind us that Nature is not an abstract realm that can be reduced to weather bulletins and wildlife documentaries on television, or scientific reports on global warming. Nature is the very substance upon which our lives are founded; the air we breathe, the water we drink, the sun that warms us, the earth that nourishes us. Our very consciousness as human beings is a sensitive interface with the vital forces of Nature. The Golden Web is a sacred network of life which is so sensitively tuned that we influence it at every turn. As we live, so we have impact on the whole. The Devas' message of unity tells us that we are all recipients of the divine breath of life and that we all belong together. To go forward together is our joint responsibility, to use the energy and simple process of our unfolding lives to maximum potential, to transform and heal the earth in all ways possible, and to help overcome the ecological crisis.

The Devas know that the way forward lies in our immediate grasp and that change can only come about through our awakening to reality as a dynamic web of relationships, of which human consciousness is an integral part. As we move beyond limitation to a more inclusive relationship with Nature, the profound expansion in thoughts, perceptions and values will bring us the inspiration to think and take positive action in our lives, to treat Nature with greater respect, to find greater compassion towards all sentient beings, to live more sustainably and in greater harmony with Nature, and to work to preserve the wild and sacred corners of the earth. It is a journey towards recognition of our full potential as human beings and the gift of life we share with all of creation. In their messages, the Devas communicate to us the divine spirit of Nature, that we may come to know it and cherish it in our own lives, and work to safeguard the precious web of life of which we are part.

# Glossary

Acupuncture

Acupuncture is a branch of traditional Chinese medicine. In the practice of acupuncture, fine needles are inserted into specific points located on energy pathways, or meridians, throughout the human body. The needles stimulate and regulate the flow of energy, or ch'i, within the meridians to bring balance to body, mind and spirit. Detailed attention is given to the diagnosis and treatment of the causes of disease, and traditional diagnosis involves observing signs of energy imbalance, depletion, and disturbance within the patient.

Angel

Angels are direct manifestations of divine consciousness and they are active in all spheres of life. They exist in their own life-stream and they assist growth and development in both the human and the Nature realms. While some levels of the angelic life-stream work closely with humanity to assist the growth of consciousness, both individually and collectively, other levels of angelic consciousness, such as the Devas, are exclusively concerned with the patterns of growth within Nature.

Angelic hierarchy

The angelic life-stream is composed of different levels of consciousness, often referred to as the 'angelic hierarchy'. Each level is composed of different vibrations of energy and reflects different aspects of divine consciousness. Each level has its own role within the divine order, and seeks to promote harmonious growth, and to bring balance to creation through its individual sphere of activity.

Biodiversity

Biodiversity is the term given to the variety of living organisms on earth and their associated processes. There are currently 1.4 million species officially recorded, out of an estimate of 30 million. While species diversity refers to the variety of individual species, genetic diversity refers to the genetic variations that lead to evolutionary change and species adaptation, as life unfolds. For every plant species that is lost, it is estimated that thirty other dependent organisms also become extinct. Loss of biodiversity is therefore cumulative in effect. It is predicted that by the year 2000 a tenth of all species will be extinct, increasing to a third by the year 2020.

Burn

    Scottish term for a small stream.

Ch'i

    Ch'i ( sometimes also written as Qi) is the Chinese term given to the energy or life-force which flows throughout Nature and throughout the human body, creating and maintaining life. Ch'i flows through the human body in connected pathways, or meridians, and is accessible at specific locations on these pathways as acupuncture points. Yin and yang are complementary aspects of ch'i energy, and the balance between these two opposing qualities of energy is essential to a good state of health.

Deva

    Devas are the archetypal energies which shape the patterns of life within the plant and mineral worlds. They belong to the angelic life-stream, and they occupy their own level of consciousness. Deva is a Sanskrit term meaning 'Shining One'. The Devas represent the many unique forms of conscious life to be found in plants, flowers, trees, vegetables, rocks, landscape, and also in the elements of earth, water, fire and air. Individually, the Devas create the specific patterns of growth of each species, and collectively they represent the pure, life-generating force to be found throughout the natural world. They are aspects of divine consciousness and they are united with the Divine at all levels.

Devic essence

Devic essence is the concentration of light and energy which is gathered to form the individual patterns of growth within Nature. When Devic essence is gathered and concentrated, it contains the blueprint or pattern of development for each species. All physical growth and formation in Nature takes place according to the patterns of growth which are shaped through Devic essence. Devic essence is fluid and active, constantly moving, changing and evolving in adaptation to existing conditions.

Ecological restoration

Ecological restoration involves the natural regeneration of ecosystems, and the process of assisting Nature to regulate and heal itself. In terms of human conservation practices, this involves the restoration of original habitats when they have been damaged, disturbed or depleted, and the preservation of the communities of living organisms that exist within them.

Elementals

The Elementals belong to the angelic life-stream, and they represent the essential forces of energy which are active in earth, water, fire and air. The Elementals are aspects of Devic consciousness and they work closely with the Devas of individual species to influence the evolving balance and order within Nature which favours life.

Gaia

Gaia is the name of the Greek Goddess of the earth in the early creation myths. The Gaia hypothesis was put forward by the scientist James Lovelock. It claimed that the life of the earth, or biosphere, is maintained in a state favourable to life by the living organisms within it. From this hypothesis evolved the Gaia theory which sees that the evolution of organisms takes place alongside the evolution of their physical and chemical environments. The biosphere therefore forms a single, evolutionary process which is entirely self-regulating.

Global warming

Global warming is the term given to the change in climate and increases of temperature generated by the build-up of atmospheric constituents known as 'greenhouse gases' which trap heat in the earth's atmosphere. Greenhouse gases include carbon dioxide, methane, chlorofluorocarbons( CFCs), nitrous oxide and ozone.The concentration of these gases in the atmosphere and the resulting overall rise in the earth's temperature is referred to as 'the greenhouse effect'.

Machair

The machair is a strip of calcareous grassland found in the shell sand dunes of the north-west Highlands and Islands of Scotland.The machair depends on a seaweed belt of spiky marram grass which stabilises the ground and protects it from erosion.The machair is developed by a colonisation of flowering plants which fix nitrogen and allow up to eighty different plant species to take root.These provide an abundant succession of flowering blooms and rich grazing for cattle and sheep.

Ozone layer

The ozone layer is in the earth's upper atmosphere and protects life on earth from harmful ultra-violet radiation. Ozone levels fluctuate monthly, but man-made pollutants such as methane, chlorine and nitrogen compounds have caused ozone depletion and a decrease in yearly average levels.

Pan

Pan is the God of the animal, vegetable, mineral and elemental kingdoms.Pan represents the cosmic energy that exists throughout Nature. In early Greek myths, Pan was depicted as half human, half animal.

Loch

Scottish term for a lake.

Nature Spirits

The Nature Spirits are the myriad beings in Nature which exist in light form. They work exclusively with the plant and mineral kingdoms to assist the fusion of Devic essence and the physical formation of plants and rocks. In traditional myths and legends, these beings were often depicted in human form and appeared as elves, fauns, gnomes and fairies in which these entities were personified. They continue to be associated with these forms to the present day.

Supramental consciousness

There are many levels of consciousness and all are structured and form different stages of the evolutionary process. The growth of individual consciousness, which includes all physical, mental, psychic and spiritual development, involves transcendence from one level to the next as each stage of growth is integrated. The mental level of consciousness involves the powers of the mind, for instance, logic, conceptual thought, rationality, analysis, and so on. The supramental level of consciousness represents the unification of individual consciousness with the Divine, where the total sum of reality is simultaneously experienced, leading to enlightenment.

# Trees for Life

Trees for Life is a charity dedicated to the regeneration of the Caledonian Forest in the Highlands of Scotland. The native pinewoods of this forest originally covered 1.5 million hectares of land, but have been reduced by human activities over the centuries to 1% of that today. In most of the scattered remnants, the forest is still declining as overgrazing by deer prevents the growth of any new trees. Most of the large mammals native to the Highlands, such as the wolf, brown bear and beaver, disappeared with their forest habitat.

Moved by the plight of this ancient forest, Trees for Life began work in 1989 to help regenerate and expand it again. Working primarily in Glen Affric, one of the best surviving fragments of the forest, we aim eventually to restore the forest to an area of 1,500 square kilometres in the north-central Highlands and reintroduce the missing species of wildlife, as they are essential parts of the forest ecosystem. Our achievements to date include the planting of over 93,500 trees, fencing 159 hectares (393 acres) of land for forest regeneration and being declared the UK Conservation Project of the Year in 1991.

For further information about our work, including our programme of volunteer work weeks in the forest, please write to:

## Trees for Life
The Park, Findhorn Bay, Forres IV36 0TZ, Scotland
tel. +44 (0)1309-691292  fax +44 (0)1309-691155
e-mail: treesforlife@gn.apc.org

# Introducing Findhorn Press

Findhorn Press is the publishing business of the Findhorn Community which has grown around the Findhorn Foundation, co-founded in 1962 by Peter and Eileen Caddy and Dorothy Maclean. The first books originated from the early interest in Eileen's guidance over 20 years ago and Findhorn Press now publishes not only Eileen Caddy's books of guidance and inspirational material, but many other books, and it has also forged links with a number of like-minded authors and organisations.

For further information about the Findhorn Community and how to participate in its programmes please write to:
The Accommodation Secretary
Findhorn Foundation
Cluny Hill College, Forres IV36 0RD, Scotland
tel. +44 (0)1309-673655  fax +44 (0)1309 673113
e-mail reception@findhorn.org

For a complete catalogue, or for more information about Findhorn Press products,
please contact :

## Findhorn Press
The Park, Findhorn, Forres IV36 0TZ , Scotland
tel. +44 (0)1309-690582 fax +44 (0)1309-690036
e-mail thierry@findhorn.org
http://www.mcn.org/findhorn/press/  or
http://www.gaia.org/gen/findhorn/press/

# Video about the Findhorn Community

STRAIGHT FROM THE HEART (£10.99)
*available in PAL and NTSC formats*
This is the latest video about the people and work of the
Findhorn Foundation, the world renowned intentional
community of people living, working and learning together in
the north east of Scotland. Through the voices and images of its
people, the story of building community is told: working with
people, eduction, ecological building and environmental work,
global networking and infusing everyday life with spiritual
values. We hope this video will touch your heart in the same
way that the Community has inspired many thousands of
people from all over the world. (31 minutes)

# Books about the Findhorn Community

SIGHTS & INSIGHTS                               isbn 1 899171 50 9
A Guide to the Findhorn Foundation Community
*Compiled by Cally and Harley Miller*

This booklet is intended to give those of you who have only
heard or read of this near-mystical place a clear and up-to-date
picture of what the Commnity is like and of what there is to see
and do here.
Illustrated with line drawings of the most striking buildings of
the Community, this booklet will take you through the various
developments of the last 34 years; it also places the Community
in its local surroundings with listings of local events, places of
interest and nature walks.

THE KINGDOM WITHIN (£8.95)          isbn 0 905249 99 2
A Guide to the Spiritual Work of the Findhorn Community
*Compiled and edited by Alex Walker*

This collection of writings about the history, work, beliefs and
practices of the Findhorn Foundation and its associated
community of spiritual seekers offers a vision of hope,
inspiration and encouragement. With contributions by David
Spangler, William Bloom, ROC, Dorothy Maclean, Peter and
Eileen Caddy amongst others, this book covers topics which
include nature and ecology, the art of living in community, the
relationship of 'new age' thought to formal religion, and co-
operation with the spiritual worlds. The world is hungry for the
hope and inspiration this book brings — and so are you!


THE FINDHORN GARDEN (£9.95)          isbn 0 905249 63 1
Pioneering a New Vision of Humanity and Nature in
Co-operation
*by The Findhorn Community*

The story of the early days of the Findhorn Community and its
communications with the nature kingdoms. Peter and Eileen
Caddy's experiences as co-founders of the community, Dorothy
Maclean's contact with the devas, R. Ogilvie Crombie's (ROC's)
meetings with Pan and the Elemental Kingdom, and the
wisdom of David Spangler and other combine to give a unique
perspective on the relationship between humans and nature.


THE FINDHORN COMMUNITY (£8.95)          isbn 0 905249 77 1
*by Carol Riddell*

The author traces the community's development over the years
and gives a clear picture of the community today and the new
businesses and independent projects springing up around it.
The second half of the book includes a number of intimate and
revealing interviews with members, both young and old, who
share their lives and experiences of living in this incredible
community.

---

*All these items can be obtained from your local bookshop,
or directly by mail order from Findhorn Press*